D1520406

# REPUBLICANS IN THE SOUTH

# REPUBLICANS IN THE SOUTH

## Voting for the State House, Voting for the White House

*Terrel L. Rhodes*

PRAEGER

Westport, Connecticut
London

**Library of Congress Cataloging-in-Publication Data**

Rhodes, Terrel L., 1949–
   Republicans in the South : voting for the State House, voting for the
White House / Terrel L. Rhodes.
     p.  cm.
   Includes bibliographical references and index.
   ISBN 0–275–96817–0 (alk. paper)
    1. Republican Party (U.S. : 1854–  ) 2. Elections—Southern States.
  3. Southern States—Politics and government—1951–  I. Title.
JK2356 .R4 2000
  324.2734′0975′09045—dc21      99–055880

British Library Cataloguing in Publication Data is available.

Library of Congress Catalog Card Number: 99–055880
ISBN: 0–275–96817–0

First published in 2000

Praeger Publishers, 88 Post Road West, Westport, CT 06881
An imprint of Greenwood Publishing Group, Inc.
www.praeger.com

Printed in the United States of America

The paper used in this book complies with the
Permanent Paper Standard issued by the National
Information Standards Organization (Z39.48–1984).

10 9 8 7 6 5 4 3 2 1

**Copyright Acknowledgment**

The author and publisher gratefully acknowledge permission for use of the following material:

Excerpts taken from Jacob E. Cooke, ed., *The Federalist*. Hanover, NH: University
Press of New England, 1961.

# Contents

*Illustrations*                                                    vii

*Preface*                                                           xi

1   Party Politics in the South                                      1

2   Southern Republican National Electoral Patterns                 19

3   The National Legislature                                        39

4   Southern State Electoral Patterns                               67

5   Indices of Party Competition                                    91

6   Party Competition in the South                                 109

*Bibliography*                                                     131

*Index*                                                            139

# Illustrations

**MAPS**

1.1  The South: The Eleven States of the Former
Confederacy                                                            14

2.1  Political Subdivisions of States by Region          26

**TABLES**

2.1  Presidential Party Support, 1920–1996              20

2.2  Southern Electoral Votes, 1900–1996               24

2.3  Presidential Primary Election Participation and
Republican Percent of Total Primary Vote,
1972–1996                                                              37

3.1  Number of Republican U.S. Senate Seats and
Contested Races, 1960–1998                                41

3.2  Percentage of Republican Vote in General Elections
for U.S. Senate, 1960–1998                               42

3.3  Total Votes Cast in Republican U.S. Senate
Primaries in the South, 1972–1998                    47

3.4    Presidential Republican Vote Gain/Loss, 1960–1964          52

3.5    Number of Republican U.S. House Seats Won in the
       South, 1968–1998                                           56

3.6    Average Percentage of Republican Vote in General
       Elections for U.S. House, 1968–1998                        58

3.7    Number of Republican Votes Cast in General
       Elections for U.S. House, 1972–1998                        60

4.1a   Number and Percent of Republican Wins in General
       Elections for Governor in the Peripheral South,
       1968–1998                                                  69

4.1b   Number and Percent of Republican Wins in General
       Elections for Governor in the Deep South,
       1967–1999                                                  70

4.2a   Number of Republican and Total State Legislative
       House of Representatives Seats in South,
       1970–1999                                                  82

4.2b   Number of Republican and Total State Legislative
       Senate Seats in South, 1970–1999                          83

4.3    Partisan Control of All State Legislative Chambers,
       1966–1999                                                  87

4.4    Republican Percentage of All State Legislative Seats
       Nationally, 1966–1999                                      88

5.1    Party Competition Based on Composite B Index              96

6.1    Gender Differences, 1992–1996                             117

**FIGURES**

2.1a   Republican Percentage of Vote for President,
       1948–1996                                                  34

2.1b   Republican and Third-Party Percentage of Vote for
       President, 1948–1996                                       35

4.1   Percentage of Republican Vote in General Elections
      for Governor, 1966–1999                                72

4.2a  Percentage of State House Seats Held by
      Republicans in the South, 1966–1999                    84

4.2b  Percentage of State Senate Seats Held by
      Republicans in the South, 1966–1999                    85

5.1   Presidential Competition Score and Category,
      1968–1996                                              95

5.2   Competition B Index Score and Category,
      1968–1998                                              98

5.3   Gubernatorial Competition Score and Category,
      1967–1999                                             101

5.4   State Legislative Lag Score                           104

5.5   State Legislative Lag Score and Category,
      1968–1999                                             105

# Preface

This book has been percolating for many years and is the result of the support and assistance of many people. I am indebted to a long line of writers and scholars who have explored the many facets of Southern politics and the growth of two-party competition in the South. Presidential Republicanism has now trickled down to the grassroots level across the South. The long-awaited realignment in Southern politics has occurred and is permanently rooted in the South. The demise of the Democratic party, though, has not occurred as some political pundits had predicted it would—it remains strong and competitive particularly at the local level and in most parts of the South.

I salute those who have labored in this arena in previous years. In particular I would like to thank Merle Black who first set me on the path of preparing this manuscript. I also acknowledge the late Frank Munger and Charles McCall, who always provided encouragement and insight when it was needed. A special thanks goes to Dr. Linda Swayne, a colleague, a rigorous critic, and a good friend who made the final product possible. As with many manuscripts, several students had a hand in the preparation of this one—Linda Hunt Williams, Bart Warner, Alex Schaunberg, and Bo King. My secretary, Amy Peacock, worked numerous hours preparing data tables. Finally, I could not have completed this project without the unwavering support of my wife, Mary, and daughters, Katie and Meghan.

# Chapter 1

# Party Politics in the South

Throughout the history of the United States, the South as a region has been a fascination for Americans economically, socially, and politically. The Civil War forged an identity for the region that persists to this day. The Southern identity has been the focus of many studies and commentaries detailing the ways in which Southerners differ from the remainder of the country—sometimes extolling the virtues of traditional values of individualism, honor, and simple gentility; sometimes decrying the perseverance of hatred, violence, and prejudice. It is the seeming continuity and persistence of contradictions that account for much of the fascination of commentators. It is not so much that these same contradictions do not exist in the rest of the country, but rather that these contradictions have been displayed in the public eye in the South in such a massive and open manner over time.

Politically, the South's distinctive identity and role in America were set during and in the wake of the Civil War—first as a pre–Civil War Democratic region in defense of Southern independence and slavery, then as a post-war Republican bastion, and then again as a solid Democratic party stronghold in reaction to the previous occupation of the federal army and the Republican party. In the heyday of the Democratic party's dominance, politics in the South became intra-party Democratic politics. Democratic partisanship dominated to the extent that participation in politics in the South became known as Southern Democracy with a capital *D*. Republicans had been relegated to small, isolated pockets in a few states of the former Confederacy where Whites had supported the forces of the Union during the Civil War, or where Blacks had not been disenfranchised when Southern Democrats returned to political power. Only gradually did Democratic party dominance begin to erode, attracting the nation's attention in the 1950s and 1960s.

The Civil War cemented in the minds of most Southerners the unremitting tie between the Republican party, the federal army, and the tyranny of Blacks and Northern carpetbaggers. The defeated South was ruled by the army and the Republican party. Democrats or anyone who had supported the secession from the Union were no longer permitted to vote. Northern patronage appointees and entrepreneurs followed the federal army to the South and took over the reins of government. Freed slaves and Blacks from Northern states accompanied Northern Whites to the South to form the small core of individuals permitted to participate in governance in the wake of the war. The Democratic party was relegated to the sidelines in most of the South. Little by little, martial law was lifted and participation by former Confederates was allowed. Finally, with the presidential election of 1876, in exchange for the White House in the contested Hayes-Tilden election, the Republicans agreed to withdraw federal troops from the South and restore civilian government, including the return of former secessionists to the political process.

With the return of the former rebels to the political arena in the South, the party of choice was the Democratic party. The abuse and profiteering that occurred under the Republican rule in the South was a strong symbol that provided a vivid motivator to support the Democratic party as the vehicle for re-establishing the South politically. One of the first orders of business was to ensure that both Blacks and Republicans, who in many areas were the same after the departure of Northern Blacks and Whites after 1876, were no longer eligible to vote in elections. Various methods of disenfranchising Republicans ensued, including poll taxes, property ownership requirements, literacy tests, and proof that a grandfather had been registered to vote. Not only Blacks, but also many poor Whites were no longer able to vote as these hurdles were formally adopted. The result was a period of Democratic allegiance and domination that extended into the middle of the twentieth century.

According to some political scientists, the political landscape in the South has now changed through a major partisan realignment of Southern voters from the Democratic to the Republican party, effecting a national advantage for Republican presidential candidates (Black and Black, *Vital South*, 1992). Others argue that what is occurring in the South is the nationalization of Southern politics. They believe that Southern politics is finally relinquishing the vestiges of the Civil War and reflecting the same basic issue positions and characteristics of the rest of the country (Phillips, 1969; Heard, 1952). Reality lies somewhere between these positions.

This book focuses on the nature of partisan competitiveness in the South both at the national and state levels of partisan electoral behavior. Throughout the twentieth century, the major emphasis in analyzing the Republican party in the South has been on "presidential" Republicanism. The strength or performance of the Republican party within individual Southern states and for state offices below the presidential level has frequently been ignored.

## POLITICAL PARTIES IN THE UNITED STATES

The examination of political parties and partisan competition requires a brief discussion of the nature and role of political parties in the United States and the competitive nature of partisan politics in setting public policy as a result of successfully electing candidates to office. Modern political parties that resemble parties as we know them today, arose in the eighteenth and nineteenth centuries during the period of democratic revolution—a period that encompassed our own revolutionary break with Great Britain. These revolutions demanded a popular voice in the workings of government. "Parties, therefore, arose as the vehicle through which the people's will could be properly registered" (Huckshorn, 1980, p. 37).

A leading scholar of American political parties, Robert Huckshorn, defined political parties in this way: "The American political party is an autonomous group of citizens having the purpose of making nominations and contesting elections in hope of gaining control over governmental power through the capture of public offices and the organization of the government" (1980, p. 13).

The definition, although general, encompasses the key elements associated with political parties wherever they are found around the world. Parties are composed of groups of people who come together to select one or more members to represent them in elections for

specified political offices so that they can direct or influence governmental actions and policies.

The primary functions associated with political parties include:

- The nomination of candidates for office
- The channeling of political struggle
- The organization of government
- The political socialization of citizens, and
- The focusing of policy concerns

Wherever political parties exist in democratic societies around
the world, they perform this set of functions for the citizens of the
country in which they are located. Through political party selection
of candidates, containment of conflict over policies within organized, peaceful processes, and coordination of governmental activities at several levels, democratic governments and societies manage
to persist.

Huckshorn further delineated six characteristics of political parties in the United States:

1. A two-party system
2. Decentralized party organization
3. Diffused party leadership
4. Lack of ideological commitment
5. Lack of responsible parties, and
6. Lack of commitment to politics

The United States' two-party tradition evolved from the British
model that dominated the thinking of the founders of the Republic.
As in Britain, American political parties emerged from groups supporting or opposing the monarchy; however, after the Revolutionary
War and independence from Britain had been achieved, supporters
of the British Crown either fled this country for Canada or other
countries, or were so few in number and support that they no longer
influenced political outcomes in any meaningful manner. The bulk
of the American population in the wake of the Revolutionary War
embraced independence and democracy. The major divisions that
occurred as a new American government was forming were over issues of centralization/decentralization, or agrarian vs. manufactur-

ing/industrial interests. Unlike the British and many European political parties, these types of issues cut across class lines in the United States, creating more heterogeneous collections of supporters for the parties that emerged after independence. In addition, the creation of a system of electoral districts that elected one member to represent the district's citizens through a plurality vote of the electorate, created a situation wherein groups had to appeal to a broad range of voters to gain sufficient votes needed for election. Appealing to narrower interests in an attempt to gain enough votes to be one of several candidates in a multi-member district was typically not an option in the American partisan political context.

In the South, the establishment of state laws requiring run-off elections if no candidate won a majority in the general election, further ensured that third parties would not flourish unless they were able to gain widespread voter allegiance quickly. With single member districts and plurality elections, unless you could win more votes than any of your rivals, you were lost. Parties and candidates that appealed to a consistent or intense minority would never win representation and thus opportunity to influence policy unless they could at the same time gain sufficient appeal to win more voters than any of their competitors. This forced major political parties to broaden their appeals to voters by taking less extreme positions, while at the same time motivating voters to support parties that espoused some of their views and had a chance of winning, even if another party represented more of their positions but had little chance of actually winning an election.

Political party organization was decentralized. Party committees existed at city, county, district, state, and national levels. These committees organized party activities and sometimes selected candidates to represent the party in the next election. Committee members and other party officers were selected by the party members in their respective city, county, or state unit, and not by a central party organization; therefore, little if any central party control could be exercised. Southern states exhibited strong county-based political organizations that tightly controlled candidate selection, voter registration, and even employment opportunities. One of the most well-known Southern state political organizations—the Byrd machine in Virginia—was built on the county courthouse organizations in rural and small-town Virginia.

As the country moved into the twentieth century, reform movements moved the parties toward primary elections that involved voters who identified themselves with a political party in the selection of the party's candidates through primary elections, further decentralizing the control of this important party function. In much of the South, the access to voting rolls remained in the hands of county courthouse politicians who resisted primary elections and greater voter participation. The rise of the Democratic party in the wake of the Reconstruction era and its efforts to thwart political involvement by African Americans through the Republican party resulted in further restriction of voter registration to White people through requirements to own property, pay taxes, or pass literacy tests. Primary participation, when it did occur, was thus mainly limited to a small number of White Democrats.

The existence of political party officers and committee members, the party candidates elected to public office, and the role of individuals who provided money to finance political candidates or party activities made it difficult in the U.S. context to clearly define who party leaders were. The republican organizational framework of government in the United States with its local, state, and national political offices and respective authority and responsibility, resulted in at least three levels of people who could claim party leadership. It was also the case in the United States, unlike in Britain, that political party officers were typically not holders of elected public office, further diffusing party leadership capabilities. It was common in the South for the county political leaders to be local business people rather than elected politicians (Hunter, 1953).

Following from the earliest post-Revolutionary days, the political consensus on individual rights and liberties, the form and function of government, and the overall political process within the United States have been pervasive. Disagreements have tended to be over the means to achieve goals and objectives within the framework of this fairly broad consensus. The lack of strong ideological commitment on the part of most of the populace resulted in the tendency for political parties to pursue moderate, or middle-of-the-road, policies and positions on issues. The resistance of political parties to espouse strong ideological positions further reinforced weak ideological positions among the general electorate and rank-and-file party identifiers. With the Northern carpetbaggers sent home after Reconstruction in the South, and most Blacks disenfranchised, there was widespread agreement on basic political ideology—government should do little except maintain the status quo.

The lack of strong ideological commitment by political parties was partially the result of a lack of a responsible party system. Autonomous party organizations selected their own candidates at local, state, and national levels, and each level of government pursued its own agendas and issues. Even when elected officials shared the same political party label, there was no central authority that was responsible for ensuring adherence to a specific, uniform party position on a given issue. Individual candidates took positions they believed would ensure that they would receive a sufficient number of votes to be re-elected in the next election, not necessarily the positions espoused by a central party committee or leader. Central committees or leaders had little power to impose penalties on party candidates or officeholders because the latter raised their own campaign money and appealed to their own voters while using the party's label. In the United States' political system, any person becomes a party member simply by declaring allegiance to the particular political party. There are no required dues, no pledge of allegiance, no background checks or sponsorship that has to occur before a person can consider himself or herself a member of the party. In most Southern states there is not even a formal party registration with the state or local elections office in order to participate in a party's primary election to select the party's candidates, so that even publicly declaring membership to a party is not necessary.

All of the factors previously discussed reflect a basic lack of commitment to politics in general that pervades American life. Jobs, family, religion, education, leisure, and a long list of other activities occupy the attention of Americans along with politics. Part of the lack of commitment to partisan politics results from the success of movements to professionalize the public bureaucracy's delivery of services so that the race, ethnicity, religion, family connection, and so on, of a person are not the determining factors for whether an individual or a family receives public services or benefits. Over time, the importance of which political party elected its candidates to public office made a noticeable difference in fewer and fewer areas of most people's lives. Americans had the luxury of ignoring partisan affiliation because important aspects of how they would be treated by government were no longer subject to arbitrary actions of individuals, or based on a person's partisan allegiance. It is estimated by political researchers that in any given year, 25 percent of the populace participates in political activities (other than voting in an election), and that only 8 percent are actually formal members of a political party or political organization (Wilson, 1992, pp. 132–134).

## PARTY COMPETITION

So why is party competition worth examining if partisan politics is of so little concern or interest to so many Americans? Whether large numbers of people actually participate or not in the political process of electing public officials in the United States, the selection of elected officials who make public policy and enact legislation affecting our lives is conducted by individuals and groups identified and supported by partisan political parties. In the United States this translates into two parties—the Republican and the Democratic parties. Based on public opinion polls of citizens, it also translates into a majority of the population identifying themselves as either Democrats or Republicans, and a majority of eligible voters voting in national presidential elections, although not necessarily in all state and local elections. Partisan politics and political parties, despite frequent criticism and skepticism, still have meaning for the American populace.

Long before the current dominant political parties existed, James Madison articulated the fundamentals of political and civil conflict and the role of competition in his defense of the U.S. Constitution and the republican form of government it created. Madison was addressing the need for the adoption of the U.S. Constitution as an enhancement to the existing national government under the Articles of Confederation. Specifically, he was addressing the need for a republican form of government in order to control factions within a democratic society. However, his conception of faction closely parallels our discussion of parties and the need for competitive forces to ensure the persistence of democratic government.

> Complaints are everywhere heard from our most considerate and virtuous citizens, equally friends of public and private faith, and of public and personal liberty; that our governments are too unstable; that the public good is disregarded in the conflicts of rival parties; and that measures are too often decided, not according to the rules of justice, and the rights of the minor party; but by the superior force of an interested and overbearing majority . . . It will be found indeed, on a candid review of our situation, that some of the distresses under which we la-

bor, have been erroneously charged on the operation of our governments . . . These must be chiefly, if not wholly, effects of the unsteadiness and injustice, with which a factious spirit has tainted our public administration.

By a faction I understand a number of citizens, whether amounting to a majority or minority of the whole, who are united and actuated by some common impulse of passion, or of interest, adverse to the rights of other citizens, or to the permanent and aggregate interests of the community. . . . (Cooke, 1961, p. 57)

Madison continued to discuss the ways in which the conflict of faction could be controlled:

There are two methods of curing the mischiefs of faction: the one, by removing its causes; the other, by controlling its effects . . . The latent causes of faction are thus sown in the nature of man . . . A zeal for different opinions concerning religion, concerning Government and many other points, as well of speculation as of practice; an attachment to different leaders ambitiously contending for pre-eminence and power; or to persons of their descriptions whose fortunes have been interesting to the human passions, have in turn divided mankind into parties, inflamed them with mutual animosity, and rendered them much more disposed to vex and oppress each other, than to co-operate for their common good.

It is in vain to say, that enlightened statesmen will be able to adjust these clashing interests, and render them all subservient to the public good. Enlightened statesmen will not always be at the helm: Nor, in many cases, can such an adjustment be made at all, without taking into view indirect and remote considerations, which will rarely prevail over the immediate interest which one party may find in disregarding the rights of another, or the good of the whole.

The inference to which we are brought, is, that the *causes* of faction cannot be removed; and that relief is only to be sought in the means of controlling its *effects*.

If a faction consists of less than a majority, relief is supplied by the republican principle, which enables the majority to defeat its sinister views by regular vote . . . When a majority is included in a faction, the form of popular government on the

other hand enables it to sacrifice to its ruling passion or interest, both the public good and the rights of other citizens. . . .

By what means is this object attainable? Evidently by one of
two only. Either the existence of the same passion or interest in
a majority at the same time, must be prevented; or the majority, having such co-existent passion or interest, must be rendered, by their number and local situation, unable to concert
and carry into effect schemes of oppression . . . If impulse and
the opportunity be suffered to coincide, we well know that neither moral nor religious motives can be relied on as an ade-
quate control. . . .

The two great points of difference between a Democracy and
a Republic are, first, the delegation of the Government, in the
latter, to a small number of citizens elected by the rest; sec-
ondly, the greater number of citizens, and the greater sphere of
country, over which the latter may be extended. (Cooke, 1961,
pp. 59–61)

Although political parties already existed at the time Madison
wrote, they did not play the extensive role they currently play in the
selection of candidates and the domination of the electoral process.
Madison's basic premise was that rule by the majority held the
seeds of its own destruction through its ability to trample on the
rights of the minority, as well as through the lack of contention over
policies and practices that could result when the majority reached a
size such that opposition to the majority could easily by over-
whelmed. Competition for the limited number of elected positions
and the competition among elected representatives from different
parts of the country—rural and urban, east and west, wealthy and
poor—would best preserve the liberty of all citizens.

Since the Democratic and Republican parties are the primary
means by which competition for elected office is organized in this
country, the importance of partisan competition warrants our focused attention. Where partisan competition does not exist, Madison would suggest that advantages would accrue from increased
competition of ideas and "passions" among the electorate within
that electoral system.

In the United States, the South has stood as the most obvious region of one-party domination during much of the twentieth century.
In a region where an overwhelming majority dominates, the explora-
tion of divergent opinions and the rights of the minority are more

likely to be abused or ignored to the detriment of the public good, according to Madison. In partisan terms this had translated into a clear minority status for Republicans in the South.

## REPUBLICANISM IN THE SOUTH

The presence of post-Civil War Southern Republicanism at the national level surfaced in the early decades of the twentieth century. As early as 1920, Southern states were voting for Republican presidential candidates and occasionally electing GOP state officials. Perhaps the most well-known and significant framing of Southern politics came from the writings of V. O. Key, Jr., beginning in the 1940s. By 1952 Alexander Heard could pose the question, *A Two-Party South?* as the title of his book. The Republican party's future in the South has been a popular topic, particularly in the aftermath of the 1964 Goldwater candidacy, Nixon's 1968 "Southern Strategy," the Reagan "Revolution" of the 1980s, and the 1994 congressional elections that resulted in Republican control of both houses of Congress for the first time in forty years.

The emphasis on "presidential" Republican vote trends and behavior has led to an underemphasis on the growth, patterns of development, and role of the party at a state level. The focus on "presidential" Republicanism is incomplete for two reasons: (1) the focus is too narrow—only one level of Republican electoral behavior is analyzed—and (2) political parties are organized on a state-by-state basis, not on a national scale regardless of the frequent "solid" presidential voting pattern among the Southern states. To present a more complete picture, this book examines the Republican party's performance in selected state level races as well as the party's presidential level of success.

One aspect of this examination will extend Pfeiffer's (1967) and David's ("How Can an Index," 1972) classic works using electoral outcomes to develop indices of party competition at the statewide level. These political scientists developed indices using presidential elections along with congressional and gubernatorial elections. The heavy reliance on presidential election outcomes, though, provided a less refined picture of the competitive position of the two major parties than measures that did not include presidential election data. The figures and indices presented here will examine the extent of party competition for statewide offices as well as presidential and congressional voting returns in order to focus on the inter-party competition within states. According to Black and Black (1992), other political commentators, and the election returns over the past seven presidential elections, the Republican party has been described as having a "lock" on the South's electoral votes. This book portends that non-presidential election returns, especially more localized, state electoral results, provide a better and different indication of the institutionalization and viability of the Republican party than do presidential voting measures, and provide a more robust insight into the nature of party realignment in the region.

Election patterns in the eleven states of the former Confederacy and the competitive position of the Republican party for the offices of president, U.S. senator and representative, governor, and state legislator will be examined. Additional measures of party strength within a state are discussed in an attempt to categorize these eleven Southern states based on the extent to which the Republican party has become a viable, competitive political force within the region.

The importance of the competitive role that the Republican party plays in a given state is not only significant for those party members within the state interested in elective offices and jobs, but also for the role of the state party within the party organization at a national level. In addition, the implications for the national role played by these eleven Southern states in the selection of the party's presidential nominee and the direction of the national parties as a result of the changing partisan landscape will be considered.

V. O. Key (*American State*, 1956, p. 110) suggested that as a minority party's chance of winning an election increases, so will intra-party competition and party factionalism. Speaking of the Democratic party's minority position in some Northern states in the early 1900s, Key's point appears to be equally applicable today for the Republican party in the South:

> As the cause of the Democratic party within the state becomes less hopeless its internal structure changes. Within the party competing centers of leadership arise. They may rest on a foundation neither more nor less substantial than the ambitions of political personalities for positions of leadership . . . As these characteristics develop they are paralleled by more frequent and more intense competition within the party among the continuing or transient centers of leadership. (1956, pp. 196–197)

Key, of course, was discussing party primaries, but this same pattern of behavior should also be exhibited in voter participation in general elections, in party primaries, and in the numbers of uncontested races for elected office. Indicators of partisan participation will be presented that reflect the growth of the Republican party.

Following the categorization of state parties on the basis of interparty competition, the examination of electoral patterns in both national and statewide races, and a look at partisan participation, some clear trends emerge that appear to be suggestive of more changes to come.

In examining the electoral patterns in the South, the focus will be on the eleven states that composed the former Confederate States of America—Alabama, Arkansas, Florida, Georgia, Louisiana, Mississippi, North Carolina, South Carolina, Tennessee, Texas, and Virginia (see Map 1.1). Although some of the more recent Southern configurations used by political analysts include such states as Oklahoma and Kentucky, which may resemble the electoral patterns of the traditional South, these states do not share the same historical experience with roots in the partisan attachments established before and especially in the wake of the Civil War. The evolution in partisan political behavior should be viewed in the context of the Civil War and Reconstruction to gather the full significance of changes that have occurred and are occurring in the South.

Within the South, there is a further subdivision that emerges in the partisan political development and evolution of electoral behavior. Six states—Arkansas, Florida, North Carolina, Tennessee, Texas, and Virginia—have historical factors that connect the partisan patterns within those states to early Republican success, thereby approximating non–Southern states to a certain degree. These states were less reliant upon the pre–Civil War plantation economy; had small, but noticeable, Republican or pro-Union pockets of people; had smaller Black populations; and experienced earlier in-migration from outside the South, especially in urban areas, than other Southern states. These six states have been called the Peripheral or Rim South. The remaining five states—Alabama, Georgia, Louisiana, Mississippi, and South Carolina—had higher proportions of African Americans, much heavier reliance on plantation economies, and resisted Republican inroads for a longer period of time, resulting in a different pattern of partisan development. These states have been referred to as Deep South states. These sub-

**Map 1.1**
**The South: The Eleven States of the Former Confederacy**

Peripheral States

Deep South States

divisions will be used to compare electoral patterns and to examine change and persistence in Southern electoral behavior.

Key identified sources of Republican strength in the South during the late 1800s and early 1900s that were established in the wake of the Civil War and Reconstruction era and persisted into more contemporary times (Key, *Southern Politics*, 1949). In three of the Peripheral South states—North Carolina, Tennessee, and Virginia—sizable pockets of "Mountain Republicans" date from the Civil War. These were literally small landowners living in the Appalachian Mountain areas of these states who did not support the secession movement at the time of the Civil War. Much smaller pockets of Mountain Republicans also existed in Arkansas, Alabama, and Georgia. The other primary source of Republican strength that emerged during the mid-1900s came from in-migration and the development of a professional middle class, especially in urban areas. In many Southern states, Northerners moved to urban areas as the space program grew, as retirement communities expanded (with the invention and widespread adoption of air conditioning), and as wealth expanded, increasing Republican partisan affiliations and forming the basis for party growth.

State-specific factors have also worked to increase Republican success. For example, in the wake of Castro's takeover of Cuba, Florida had a strong urban surge of Cuban immigrants who identified with the national Republican party because it had supported the ousted Cuban government that they had supported. However, the growth of urban Republicanism was never enough to create serious two-party statewide competition in most Southern states. It has been the rural, native White Southerners' switch to the Republican party, emerging most strongly in the Deep South states, that has been the basis for what could be termed a more traditional partisan realignment.

## ORGANIZATION OF THE BOOK

Early partisan electoral patterns will be presented to position the Southern states historically and to demonstrate variations in Republican strength. The next chapter will focus on presidential electoral patterns in the South, particularly since 1968. Southern presidential voting patterns show the earliest departures from support of the Democratic party. Even though some Southern states voted for Republican presidential candidates as early as 1920, they have been susceptible to third party candidates as well—much more than the rest of the country. Supporting third party candidates appears to have been generally more acceptable to many Southern voters than voting for a Republican presidential candidate.

Chapter 3 examines Southern electoral support for U.S. Senate and House of Representatives candidates. Senate candidates are elected statewide, but are frequently associated more closely with national issues and their national party than any other officials elected at the state level. On the other hand, although members of the House are national politicians, enacting national policies, they are elected from sub-state districts. U.S. representatives are much more likely to be able to distance themselves from national party positions and issues by their concentration on issues and projects designed for their local district and its voters. The electoral outcomes of House races provide another indicator of party competition on a state-by-state basis.

Chapter 4 focuses on the election of Southern governors, who are the most visible political officeholders in a state. Governors typically rise through the ranks of party offices in a state, are associated with issues and events within a state, and are more likely to be known by voters within a state not only as a party's candidate, but also as a person the voters have been able to witness for a period of time in different settings within the state. Since governors are focused on statewide issues, they are also more likely than either presidents or congressional candidates to reflect basic voter allegiances within a state.

Although the governor may be the most visible public official in a state, in Southern states historically, governors' offices are not powerful positions. In most Southern states during most of the twentieth century, the state legislature has been the political institution where the formal power in a state has resided. Governors have typically had very limited power to appoint officials or to act in the absence of state legislative authorization or permission. State constitutions typically invest governmental power for raising and spending money, formulating public policy, and determining electoral procedures and structures in their state legislatures. Therefore, the success of a political party and its relative competitiveness statewide will be most revealed at the state legislative level. In addition, state legislative candidates are most likely to be known by their voters, to be "like" the people who are electing them, and to be reflective of local issues rather than international, national, or even many statewide issues. State legislative election outcomes provide the clearest picture of the relative strength of political parties within a state that can be easily aggregated on a statewide basis.

Chapter 5 presents indices of party competition within the Southern states at various levels of electoral politics. Competition at the presidential, national legislative, gubernatorial, and state legislative levels is examined. The final chapter discusses other factors that have influenced the changing electoral patterns in the South and the prospects for future developments based on partisan competitive behavior in the latter part of the twentieth century. Through the examination of these recent patterns of competition in national and state level elections, questions of both two-party competition in the South and party realignment can be addressed more fully. Two-party competition now exists across the South at both presidential and national legislative levels. Statewide in the South, two-party competition also exists for gubernatorial elections, although not on as pervasive a scale or for as long as on the presidential level. At the most local level examined here—state legislatures—competition continues to lag behind the two-party trend in most Southern states. Although the Republican party has become more competitive even at this more local level in all Southern states, it has a long way to go before it is truly competitive with the Democratic party throughout the South.

As the population of the states in the South has become more reflective of the nation through in-migration from other parts of the country, through the pervasive spread of national media, and through the changes that have occurred in the wake of the Civil Rights era of the 1960s, Southern politics has become nationalized. In other words, Southern politics has become more like politics in the rest of the country in terms of both access and participation. At the same time, as the Republican party has grown in the South and provided a strong basis for Republican control of the White House and the Congress, the importance of Southern voters and their support, and the influence of Southern politicians and their preferences, have increased within the Republican party and therefore have become more influential in national agenda setting and policy formulation. There is divergence in party competition among the Southern states and among levels of elective office, challenging the 'solid' South perception. Not only has the Republican party become very successful in the South in recent elections, a full-blown, traditional partisan realignment can now be argued to have occurred.

When the Democrats were dominant in the South, Southerners played a similar role within the national Democratic party and the nation as they do now in the Republican party. As Southern politics has become more like the national patterns, national politics has become Southernized through the predominance of Southern Republican politicians in elected positions within Congress and the presidency. When the Republican party gained control of Congress in 1994 for the first time in forty years, the victory resulted heavily from the success of the party in Southern states. Their continued control after 1994 rested on the majority they held in congressional seats in the South; whereas the Democrats held a majority in the remainder of the country. Four of the seven presidents from 1964 to 1996 have either been from Southern states (Johnson, Carter, Clinton), or have claimed Southern roots (Bush). In many ways from the middle of the twentieth century to the end of the century, we have come full circle in terms of the role the South plays in national politics.

*Chapter 2*

# Southern Republican National Electoral Patterns

At the national level the South was indeed a solid Democratic electoral region for most of the period from 1876 to 1948. Only in 1920 and 1928 did any Southern state record its electoral votes for a Republican presidential candidate. During the first two-thirds of this century, only Tennessee elected a Republican governor (1910, 1912, 1920), no state elected a Republican senator and only Tennessee, North Carolina, Texas, and Virginia (all Peripheral South states) sent a Republican to the House of Representatives.

## PRESIDENTIAL ELECTIONS

In presidential elections in the latter third of the twentieth century, the South became increasingly susceptible to Republican incursions. Table 2.1 illustrates the number of times and the years in which Southern states have voted non-Democratic. Although not appreciated at the time, the 1948 election signaled the first large-scale break with Southern Democracy at the presidential level. After the 1948 election in which several Southern Democratic state parties—the Dixiecrats as they were called—refused to support the national Democratic ticket because of the party's position on racial integration, the solid Democratic South at the national level was no more. Even in 1948, some of the third-party success was related to

**Table 2.1**
**Presidential Party Support, 1920–1996**

| YEAR | 1920 | 1924 | 1928 | 1932 | 1936 | 1940 | 1944 | 1948 | 1952 | 1956 | 1960 | 1964 | 1968 | 1972 | 1976 | 1980 | 1984 | 1988 | 1992 | 1996 |
|---|---|---|---|---|---|---|---|---|---|---|---|---|---|---|---|---|---|---|---|---|
| **STATE** | | | | | | | | | | | | | | | | | | | | |
| **Peripheral** | | | | | | | | | | | | | | | | | | | | |
| Arkansas | | | | | | | | | | | | | | | | | | | | |
| Florida | | | | | | | | | | | | | | | | | | | | |
| N. Carolina | | | | | | | | | | | | | | | | | | | | |
| Tennessee | | | | | | | | | | | | | | | | | | | | |
| Texas | | | | | | | | | | | | | | | | | | | | |
| Virginia | | | | | | | | | | | | | | | | | | | | |
| **DEEP** | | | | | | | | | | | | | | | | | | | | |
| Alabama | | | | | | | | | | | | | | | | | | | | |
| Georgia | | | | | | | | | | | | | | | | | | | | |
| Louisiana | | | | | | | | | | | | | | | | | | | | |
| Mississippi | | | | | | | | | | | | | | | | | | | | |
| S. Carolina | | | | | | | | | | | | | | | | | | | | |

| | |
|---|---|
| Republican | |
| Other | |
| Democrat | |

the ability of the Dixiecrat party to "capture" the Democratic label on the ballot, thus gaining some votes of traditional Democratic voters who were unaware that they were not supporting the regular Democratic ticket. In 1956, for the first time, a majority of Southern electoral votes were in the Republican column. In only three more elections would the South be solid in its support of a presidential party—1972, 1984, and 1988—all of them were Republican sweeps.

Eisenhower's national war hero candidacy in 1952 and 1956 parlayed the traditional Republican strength in some Peripheral South states with a growing urban Republicanism into GOP victories in the South for the first time in nearly thirty years.

Voting patterns also suggest that the 1964 Goldwater candidacy had a major influence on traditional voting patterns in the South. In the Deep South, Goldwater's candidacy broke new ground in presidential voting patterns for Republican candidates. However, Goldwater's candidacy interrupted the Republican trend in three of the Peripheral states—Florida, Tennessee, and Virginia—that had voted Republican in the three previous elections. These states returned to the Republican column in 1968 and in 1972. It is entirely possible that these states would have voted for fellow Southerner, Lyndon Johnson, even if the Republicans had nominated someone else. Most important, the Goldwater candidacy disrupted the traditional rural, White attachment to the Democratic party in Deep South states. Just as Southern White, Deep South voters had bolted the national Democratic party in 1948 for Strom Thurmond's Dixiecrat party because of the national party's stand on racial policies, so too did Goldwater's 1964 campaign, with its different, more subtle racial appeal, prompt White Southerners in Deep South states to desert the national Democratic party again. In addition, his candidacy withheld Republican votes in Peripheral states, resulting in further weakening of traditional party allegiances in general. During this same time, African American voters for the first time overwhelmingly voted for the Democratic presidential nominee; a practice that has continued to the present time.

The evidence indicates that White Democrats provided the huge majorities for Goldwater in the five Southern states he carried. The Republican vote rose in Southern "Black Belt" counties, counties that gained their name from the rich, black soil and their large plantation economies, and that resulted historically in majority Black populations in these areas. The Republican vote also increased in rural, traditionally Democratic areas, but fell in traditionally Republican areas—urban areas in the Peripheral South, and in Black precincts (Cosman, *Five States*, 1967, p. 13). Cosman points out that increased Black voting in 1964, which was overwhelmingly against Goldwater, probably provided the winning margin for Johnson in some states such as North Carolina.

Following the 1964 and 1968 elections, the effectiveness of the Goldwater campaign approach, which was primarily the same approach that George Wallace pursued in challenging the Democratic party leadership from within the party, but in a different, racially moderated clothing, was clearly effective in winning White votes in the South. It was a key to success—at least at the presidential level—for a Republican South. A conservative Republican candidate's appeal to basic individual and states' rights positions along with a strong undercurrent of race could mobilize enough White voters to carry most Southern states for a Republican candidate.

As Table 2.1 indicates, the year 1948 clearly marked the beginning of a new pattern in the South with regard to presidential voting behavior. Since 1948 no fewer than four states have defected from Democratic allegiance to the Republican or a third-party candidate every quadrennial presidential election, culminating in the 1968 election when only one state—Texas—remained in the Democratic column. In 1972 the South became solid once again—a solid Republican South. After 1972, in only one election (1976) did the majority of Southern states record their electoral votes for a Democratic presidential candidate.

Although the importance of the South to the Democratic presidential candidate had been declining as the Democrats captured more of the previously Republican Northeast and Midwest regions during the 1930s, the significance of support from the Democratic South for the national Democratic party did not become glaringly apparent until the 1960s/1970s. It became clear to Democrats that they could not discount the South for three basic reasons: (1) Southern electoral votes can determine the difference between victory and defeat for the Democratic presidential candidate (in 1916 during the Republican era, in 1948 when the South gave Truman the needed electoral college majority, and in 1976 when Jimmy Carter was elected); (2) the proportion of the electoral votes and congressional seats from Southern states has increased (indeed the South may hold the electoral balance as the number of electoral votes from Southern states increases and the Democratic party strives to become competitive in traditionally Republican areas outside the

South); and (3) the Democratic party still enjoys at least the nominal plurality support and dominance in party registration and office holding in a majority of the Southern states. In other words, there still exists a Democratic majority base within most Southern states at the sub-presidential level that needs to be cultivated and preserved if the party is to be successful at the presidential level.

## ELECTORAL VOTE STRATEGIES

Presidential election strategies focus on states because under the electoral system embodied in the U.S. Constitution, presidents are elected on the basis of electoral votes that are won on a state-by-state basis. The total number of electoral votes is equal to the number of representatives in the U.S. House of Representatives (435 electoral votes), the number of senators in the U.S. Senate (100 electoral votes), and 3 electoral votes allocated to the District of Columbia for a total of 538 electoral votes. The District of Columbia received 3 electoral votes for the first time in 1964 through the ratification of Amendment XXIII to the U.S. Constitution (1961). Congress has set the total number of representatives at 435 in the House, and the Constitution sets 100 as the number of Senate seats. Therefore, to win the presidency, a candidate must win a majority—270 votes—of the total 538 electoral votes possible.

Southern electoral votes (representing over 31 percent of the total electoral votes available) have not been critical to the Republicans, although they do give the Republican party a head start on presidential elections that was previously enjoyed by the Democratic party. However, Southern electoral votes have made the difference between winning and losing for the Democratic candidate as recently as 1976 (see Table 2.2). After the 2000 Census the expectation is that the South as a region will gain electoral votes at the expense of the Northeast, Midwest, and Plains regions. The gains however will not be uniform. Although it is expected that Florida, Georgia, and Texas may gain electoral votes, Mississippi may actually lose votes.

Because the South is the single largest block in the Republican strategic base, carrying the South becomes even more important in the future as it gains electoral votes after the national 2000 Census. In addition, a "trickle down" effect in partisan politics in the South increasingly provides the Republican party with a foundation for control of Congress and state level offices that previously had been a

**Table 2.2**
**Southern Electoral Votes, 1900–1996**

| Year | Democrats | Republicans | Other | Total Winner Plurality | South Made Difference For Winner |
|------|-----------|-------------|-------|------------------------|----------------------------------|
| 1900 | 112 |     |    | 137 |           |
| 1904 | 120 |     |    | 196 |           |
| 1908 | 120 |     |    | 159 |           |
| 1912 | 126 |     |    | 347 |           |
| 1916 | 126 |     |    | 23  | 1916 Dem. |
| 1920 | 114 | 12  |    | 77  |           |
| 1924 | 126 |     |    | 246 |           |
| 1928 | 64  | 62  |    | 357 |           |
| 1932 | 124 |     |    | 415 |           |
| 1936 | 124 |     |    | 515 |           |
| 1940 | 124 |     |    | 367 |           |
| 1944 | 127 |     |    | 333 |           |
| 1948 | 88  |     | 39 | 75  | 1948 Dem. |
| 1952 | 71  | 57  |    | 353 |           |
| 1956 | 61  | 67  | 1  | 384 |           |
| 1960 | 79  | 33  | 16 | 84  |           |
| 1964 | 81  | 47  |    | 434 |           |
| 1968 | 25  | 57  | 46 | 111 |           |
| 1972 |     | 129 | 1  | 504 |           |
| 1976 | 118 | 11  | 1  | 57  | 1976 Dem. |
| 1980 | 12  | 118 |    | 443 |           |
| 1984 |     | 138 |    | 512 |           |
| 1988 |     | 138 |    | 314 |           |
| 1992 | 39  | 108 |    | 202 |           |
| 1996 | 51  | 96  |    | 220 |           |

*Sources: Guide to U.S. Elections;* Scammon, *America Votes*

mainstay of Democratic dominance in the national legislative arena. As the South grows, it plays a larger role in each party's strategy for winning the White House. Throughout most of its history, the South as a region has voted together for presidential candidates. No Democrat has won the White House without carrying at least some Southern states.

It is evident from the data and from general observations, that the South is no longer a solid Democratic source of electoral support at the national level. Indeed, Black and Black (*Politics and Society*, 1987; *Vital South,* 1992) have argued that at least at the presidential level, the South is now a Republican stronghold. Since 1972, with the one exception in 1976, the Republicans have won a majority of Southern electoral votes. The Democratic party, though, has not faded away as many predicted. After two back-to-back sweeps

(1984 and 1988) of the Southern electoral votes by the GOP, the Democrats won respectively 27 percent and 35 percent of the South's electoral votes in 1992 and 1996.

Although various political analysts divide the country into geographic regions somewhat differently, regional patterns do emerge when examining political behavior. For example, *Congressional Quarterly* (*CQ*) divides the country into six regions based on shared background, economy, and political tradition. In its categorization, Oklahoma, Kentucky, and West Virginia are included in the South although they were not part of the former Confederacy. Based on settlement patterns, economy, and tradition, they are more similar (in the *CQ* authors' estimation) to the South than other adjacent regions. The important point is that although some states might be argued into or out of a particular region, there are regional electoral patterns that are used by candidates of both parties as a basis for development of strategies for winning the White House.

The *CQ* regions are (see Map 2.1):

*South* (Alabama, Arkansas, Florida, Georgia, Kentucky, Louisiana, Mississippi, North Carolina, Oklahoma, South Carolina, Tennessee, Texas, Virginia, and West Virginia) with a total of 168 electoral votes or 31 percent of the total electoral votes, and 62 percent of the 270 needed to win the presidency (the traditional South of the Confederacy yields 147 electoral votes or 31 percent of the total votes, and 54 percent of the number needed to win the presidency).

*East* (Connecticut, Delaware, District of Columbia, Maine, Maryland, Massachusetts, New Hampshire, New Jersey, New York, Pennsylvania, Rhode Island, and Vermont) with a total of 122 electoral votes or 23 percent of the total, and 46 percent of the total needed to win.

*Midwest* (Illinois, Indiana, Iowa, Michigan, Minnesota, Missouri, Ohio, and Wisconsin) with 112 electoral votes or 21 percent of the total, and 42 percent of the number needed to win.

*Plains* (Kansas, Nebraska, North Dakota, and South Dakota) with 17 electoral votes or 3 percent of the total, and 6 percent of the number needed to win.

*Mountain* (Alaska, Arizona, Colorado, Idaho, Montana, Nevada, New Mexico, Utah, and Wyoming) with 43 electoral votes or 8 percent of the total, and 16 percent of the number needed to win.

*Pacific* (California, Hawaii, Oregon, and Washington) with 76 electoral votes or 14 percent of the total, and 28 percent of the number needed to win the presidency.

Map 2.1
Political Subdivisions of States by Region

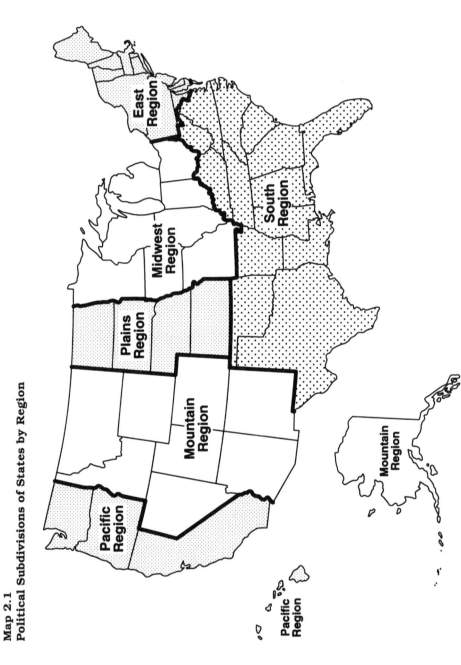

As previously indicated, one can quibble with the divisions of the regions; however, if we examine regional voting patterns over time, there are partisan patterns that emerge. Focusing on the presidential elections in 1992 and 1996, a shift in regional partisan support has occurred. Just as the South has shifted from its historical pattern as a one-party Democratic presidential region to a one-party Republican presidential region in recent years, the East and Midwest have shifted from predominantly one-party Republican presidential regions to predominantly one-party Democratic regions. If these patterns persist, and clearly the major political parties recognize these shifts, the Republicans will increasingly rely upon winning virtually all of the South's electoral votes, as well as the Plains states and the Mountain states (a total of 228 electoral votes, or 84 percent of the number needed to win), whereas the Democrats will rely upon carrying the East and Midwest (a total of 234 electoral votes, or 87 percent of the total needed to win). The Pacific region, and in particular California, becomes a critical key to an electoral victory. Either party could win without California if it ran well in the remainder of the country, but California can make the difference if the parties hold the bulk of their regions of strength. California itself holds 10 percent of the total electoral votes (54 electoral votes), and 20 percent of the number needed to win the presidency, and this will increase after the 2000 Census. Included in the national strategy for both parties is the goal to chip away specific states in the other party's electoral bases of strength.

## SOUTHERN PRESIDENTIAL CANDIDATES

Since 1960 Democratic success in the South appears to be closely tied to having a presidential nominee from the South. In 1964 (Johnson), 1976 (Carter), 1980 (Carter), 1992 (Clinton), and 1996 (Clinton), the Democratic presidential nominee was from a Southern state and the Democratic nominee was elected four of those five times. When the Democratic nominee has been from a Northern state, as in 1968 (Humphrey), 1972 (McGovern), 1984 (Mondale), and 1988 (Dukakis), the Democratic nominee has lost, and in only one of those elections (Humphrey in 1968) did the nominee receive *any* electoral votes in the South.

The need to have a presidential candidate from the South does not appear to exist for Republican presidential nominees. During this same time period, Republican presidential candidates came from Midwestern states (Ford in 1976 and Dole in 1996), losing both elections, or Western states (Goldwater in 1964, Nixon in 1968 and 1972, and Reagan in 1980 and 1984), winning four of five times. Only with George Bush in 1988 and 1992 did the GOP nominee lay claim to a Southern home state (Texas), and that nominee lost one of two elections.

In the 2000 presidential election, both parties may have candidates from Southern states. The GOP's leading candidate is George W. Bush, governor of Texas and son of former Republican President George Bush. The Democrat's favored candidate is Vice President Al Gore of Tennessee, although he is challenged by former Senator Bill Bradley of New Jersey. Both front-runner candidates are considered to be from the more moderate center of their respective parties.

## PARTISAN TRENDS IN THE SOUTH

A majority of Southern voters still appears to cling to past patterns of mistrust of "national" Democrats who are not aligned with Southerners' positions on many issues. Republican candidates are often perceived as representing positions that are at least closer to a majority of White Southerners' views.

Nationally, the Democratic party has won a majority of the presidential vote only five times since the Civil War: the four Franklin Roosevelt elections (1932, 1936, 1940, and 1944) and the Johnson election (1964). This suggests that White voters nationally favor the Republican candidate or a third-party candidate (i.e., their allegiance to the Democratic party is less fixed than in previous electoral periods). The heavily Democratic vote among African American voters is not enough to offset Republican preferences among White voters at the national level. However, presidential elections are not determined by popular vote, but rather by state electoral votes. Therefore, a massive shift in partisan preference among White voters in Southern and Western/Plains states may not be as visible in affecting presidential outcomes because of counter shifts or smaller shifts concentrated in other states that may hold larger electoral vote totals. Even though the Republican party has enjoyed strong success at the presidential level throughout most of the latter twentieth century, the 1992 and 1996 elections indicate that with the right combination of candidates and issues the Democrats at the presidential level can assemble a winning national strategy.

In the 1992 and 1996 presidential elections, Bill Clinton and the Democratic party broke the Republican trend in the South. In both elections a third-party campaign was waged by Ross Perot, a Southerner. Perot's candidacy garnered 19 percent of the presidential vote in 1992, dropping to 8 percent in 1996, but resulted in no electoral votes either time. In his best year (1992) Perot ran poorest in the South, gaining only 7 percent of the Black vote and 15 percent of the White fundamentalist Christian vote. Whites in the South, on the whole, maintained an allegiance to the Republican nominee at the presidential level, placing 108 of the South's 1992 electoral votes in the GOP column and only 39 in the Democratic party column (*Congressional Quarterly*, Nov. 7, 1992).

The three-way 1992 election witnessed the biggest increase in voter turnout since 1952, and with 55 percent of the eligible voters voting it was the highest total turnout since 1968. Part of this increase was accounted for by an increase in first-time voters who cast 11 percent of the votes in 1992. Part of the Democratic success in 1992 can be linked to these first-time voters who voted 48 percent for the Democratic candidate, 30 percent for the Republican nominee, and 22 percent for Perot (*Congressional Quarterly*, Nov. 7, 1992). Nationally, Clinton managed to revive much of the earlier Democratic coalition of the New Deal era. Republicans not only witnessed the loss of some groups of voters that had supported them in the past, including union members and younger voters, but also experienced disruption of the Republican base of support in the suburbs (e.g., Clinton carried 17 of the 28 suburban counties with populations of 500,000 or more in 1992—counties that had previously supported Republican candidates).

Although in 1996 there was also a three-way race that included Perot, his support evaporated in most of the country in 1996 as opposed to four years earlier, but was sufficient to keep any candidate from winning a majority of the popular vote. In contrast to 1992, the voter turnout at 49 percent in 1996 was the lowest since 1924 (Cook, *Congressional Quarterly*, Jan.18, 1997, pp. 185–187). Clinton made further inroads into the Republican areas in much of the country. He ran stronger in the suburbs than in 1992, recording the best results since 1964 for the Democrats; he increased the Democratic percentage of the vote in small industrial towns, in rural areas in the South and the Plains states, and among minority voters; he also managed to win a majority of the Catholic vote. As a result of the decrease in the Perot vote, the 1996 Republican vote increased over its 1992 vote, but on the whole the Democratic increases out-stripped Republican gains in most geographic areas (Cook, *Congressional Quarterly*, Dec. 21, 1996). Clinton ran the strongest in the urban areas of the Frost Belt, the Sun Belt, and the Pacific west.

The decline in Republican dominance at the presidential level in the 1990s is reflected in shifting regional voting patterns; for example, as Republicans strengthened their electoral base in the Plains, Mountains, and South, the Democrats were improving their performance in the Northeast, Midwest, and the Pacific coast states. In 1996, Clinton received the third highest number of votes for a winning presidential candidate. As the solid Republican South was disappearing in the 1990s, for the first time since the 1920 and 1924 elections, the Northeast voted as a block for a presidential candidate. Unlike the earlier period, this time it was a solid Democratic block. Clinton carried every Midwest state except Indiana, and he increased his Southern electoral vote total to 51 votes. The 1992 and 1996 Republican percentage of the popular vote was the lowest back-to-back level of presidential vote since the 1930s. Clinton carried 31 states, 18 with a majority of the vote (compared to only Arkansas and the District of Columbia in 1992), including 2 states in the South (Arkansas and Louisiana). For the Republicans, Dole carried only 19 states and only 6 with a majority; and only 1 of those was a Southern state (Alabama). Unlike Bush in 1992, who ran strongest in the South as a region, Dole in 1996 ran strongest in the Plains and Mountain states (Cook, *Congressional Quarterly*, Jan. 18, 1997).

In view of the fact that Democrats have improved their performance in traditionally Republican areas in the Northeast and Midwest, the importance of the Republican base in the South becomes more critical as part of a Republican national strategy to win the White House and Congress. The difficulty for Democrats is that their advantage is increasing in areas that have either been losing population or growing at a slower rate than the areas where Republican gains have been occurring (e.g., the South). Just as the growth in Republican voters in the South and Sun Belt in general has been boosted by immigration from the Frost Belt, the Frost Belt has become more Democratic at the presidential level. The same can be said about the trends that have emerged in the suburban areas in the 1992 and 1996 elections. Many Republican voters have been moving to newer, fringe suburbs, being replaced by more Democratic voters, including minorities, moving from the urban core.

Therefore, part of what might appear to be partisan shifts is in reality the movement of people who take their partisan preferences with them from one geographic area to another.

The overall presidential position of the Republican party has declined. In 1992, for the first time since the 1932 Hoover-Roosevelt election, a Democratic presidential candidate defeated an incumbent Republican president and then succeeded in getting re-elected. In 1996, for the second election in a row the GOP lost the presidency. In both elections, in one of the Republican party's strongest regions of support, the Democrats carried 4 Southern states, increasing their 1996 share to over a third of the South's electoral votes. A majority of the Catholic vote, a key Reagan-Democrat constituency in the 1980s, returned to the Democratic column in 1996.

It is not clear how much of the 1992 and 1996 election results are a reflection of partisan shifts or the individual candidates involved. Rapaport suggests that "the impact of a popular or unpopular nominee is more than a short-term perturbation in the long-term factor of party identification, and the effect cannot be captured entirely by issues. Favorable and unfavorable views of parties (as expressed in partisanship) are linked to voter views of parties' nominees. This analysis makes it clear why parties find it hard to recover fully from under the shadow of their unpopular predecessors" (1997, p. 197).

Miller and Shanks found that White voters who came of voting age between 1969 and 1976 exhibited strong unaligned partisan affiliations. During the Reagan presidency, these same voters exhibited a resurgence of partisanship toward the Republican party. Not since Franklin Roosevelt had this pattern arisen to this extent. "A detailed analysis of the realignment of the Reagan years . . . indicates two quite distinct stages of change in which Reagan's personal leadership and then his partisan ideology first moved the younger, less politicized voters and then the older, more politicized ones into the Republican party" (1996, p. 145).

As it relates to realignment, Beck ("A Socilization Theory," 1974) and Carmines and Stimson (1991) have found that in terms of age, the years from 18 to 30 comprise the most important period of partisan change. With 11 percent of the votes in 1992 being cast by first-time voters and only 30 percent of them voting Republican, an uninterrupted eight years of a Democratic presidency may presage longer-term problems for continued presidential dominance by the Republican party. Despite multiple, highly publicized investigations into wrongdoing involving the president and actual impeachment by the U.S. House of Representatives, high levels of approval persist related to the job performance of the president as reflected in national public opinion polls. A whole new group of voters is coming of partisan age in an era of Democratic success at the presidential level.

Preliminary indications are that Clinton has had the same if not more impact on party identification and change as Reagan. Bush was not able to provide the same impetus to the growth of Republican identifiers as Reagan was. However, what is most surprising is the influence of Clinton on party choice in the 1990s. It appears that any president popular enough to win two elections to office may well be able to sway partisan attachments during a period of "candidate-centered" politics (Parker and Copa, 1998).

The South, notwithstanding, remains a heavily Republican area in presidential elections despite these Democratic accomplishments, although it is not a Republican "lock" for presidential candidates. It does appear, however, that Democrats will do best if they nominate a Southerner as their presidential candidate if they want to peel away some Southern electoral votes.

Prior to 1968, Republican inroads in the South had tended to be in Peripheral South states, but in 1964, states that had never voted Republican overwhelmingly supported the Goldwater candidacy. However, the candidacy of George Wallace in 1968 temporarily siphoned many voters in these states away from both of the major party nominees. In examining presidential voting in the South since 1968, a distinctive pattern emerges.

The 1972 election is a useful point for focusing an examination of contemporary Republican strength in the South for several reasons: (1) the 1972 election is the first election since the full Republican breakthrough in the Deep South wherein Democrats and Republicans went head-to-head without a major third-party candidate in the race; (2) the 1972 election is the first presidential election after the passage of the Voting Rights Act of 1965 in which its full impact was witnessed—for the first time in 1972 in the South, African Americans were registered and able to vote in large numbers in a presidential election without race being a blatant focus; (3) Richard Nixon and the Republican party openly pitched their election strategy to the South to win the White House in an effort to attract both the Goldwater and Wallace voters of 1964 and 1968 but without the obvious racial appeals; (4) it is the first election wherein the Republican party swept the electoral votes of the Southern states, creating a solid South under the GOP banner.

As the discussion of the success of the Republican party in the Deep South and the Peripheral South states has suggested, the earliest Republican inroads in the South tended to be in Peripheral South states. The 1964 election witnessed the first major success for the party in the Deep South with a noticeable decline in support in the Peripheral South.

Figures 2.1a and 2.1b reveal that the traditional distinction between the Deep South and Peripheral South states in their presidential voting behavior has basically disappeared. In Figure 2.1a, the Republican percentage of the vote in these sub-regions is nearly the same during the post-1968 period. In the elections from 1972 through 1988, the Republican dominance is complete. Over this sixteen-year period, every Southern state averages a majority of its votes for the Republican nominee although Jimmy Carter captured every Southern state but one in 1976. Beginning in 1972, the Deep South became more supportive of the Republican party than the Peripheral South states with the exception of 1976 and 1980 when Carter's home state of Georgia skewed the Deep South totals. The Republican ascendance is uniform and complete. Even when the 1992 and 1996 Democratic presidential victories of Clinton are added to the equation, the Republican mean percentage of the vote during this most recent twenty-four-year period (starting from 1972) remains above 50 percent in every Southern state except Clinton's home state of Arkansas.

Figure 2.1b combines the Republican and third-party votes for a total non-Democratic vote in Southern states. Even though voter support for third-party candidates does not translate automatically into support for Republican candidates in other elections, Figure 2.1b clearly demonstrates the weakness of the core Democratic vote in Southern states in both the Peripheral and Deep South states. It also demonstrates the huge impact of the Dixiecrats in Deep South states in 1948, and the similar and smaller response to a third party in the 1992 and 1996 elections in both the Peripheral and Deep South states—the Republican allegiance was firmly established across the South.

Average partisan vote over a series of elections masks many other factors; but the overwhelming response of Southern voters to Republican nominees during this period is clearly illustrated by focusing on mean vote percentages. In terms of two-party competitiveness in the South, the two most recent Democratic showings (1992 and 1996) move the contest for Southern voters into a two-party

# Figure 2.1a
## Republican Percentage of Vote for President, 1948–1996
(Third-Party listed below election year)

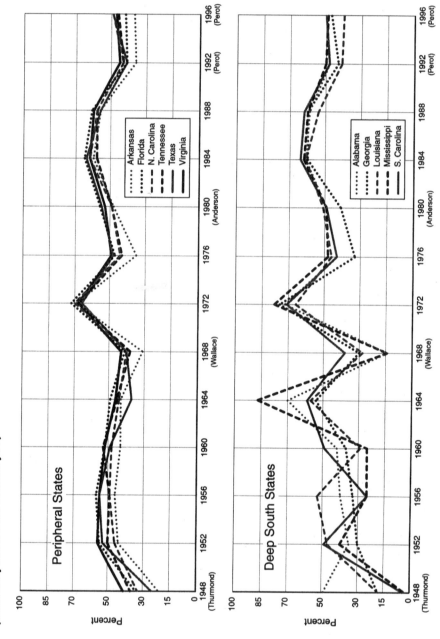

# Figure 2.1b
## Republican and Third-Party Percentage of Vote for President, 1948–1996
(Third-Party candidate listed below election year)

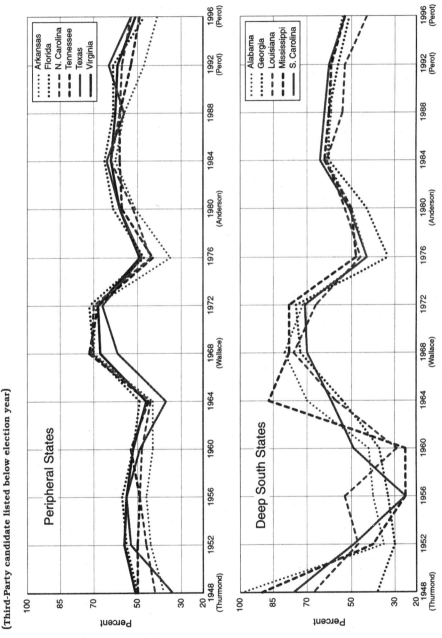

competitive position. On the other hand, the recent elections may simply be "a blip" in a Republican trend across the South.

Three of the four states—Arkansas, Tennessee, and Georgia—whose average Republican vote falls below the mean for the South in both the 1972–1988 and the 1972–1996 periods, are not simply an electoral accident; they are the home states of the Democratic candidates in 1976, 1980, 1992, and 1996. The 1972 through 1988 columns on Table 2.1a give an indication of the "typical" vote in Arkansas and Tennessee without Clinton and Gore, while dropping Georgia out of the calculation in 1976 and 1980, when Carter headed the Democratic ticket, increases the Georgia mean Republican vote to 57 percent. At the presidential level, the Republican party is the party to beat in the South. The most recent elections suggest, though, the potential Republican weakness in the South when the Democrats nominate candidates from the South for president or vice president.

The presence of favorite sons in Georgia and Arkansas has had an impact in delaying the movement of these states into a firmer Republican direction. The Republican capture of the congressional delegations in both states in 1994/96, and the close wins or losses of Democratic Senate and gubernatorial candidates in 1994/96/98, signal the convergence of these states into the overall Southern Republican trend. The fact that Bush lost Georgia in 1992 and Dole narrowly carried it in 1996 further suggests the erosion of Democratic strength in Georgia.

The presence of George Bush on the GOP ticket in 1992 and 1996 helped hold Texas strongly in the Republican column. If Governor George W. Bush is the party's candidate in 2000, this electoral vote-rich state will remain in the Republican camp. On the other hand, the Republican loss of Florida in 1996 for the first time since 1976 suggests that Republican voting patterns among some groups of voters, for example, retirees and younger Cuban American voters, can be influenced with the right candidates and issues (Scicchitano and Scher, 1997, p. 242).

## PRESIDENTIAL PRIMARIES

Another piece of evidence that indicates the growth of the presidential Republican presence in the South is the participation of voters in presidential primaries. Participation in primaries is subject to wide variation depending on such factors as whether an incumbent

**Table 2.3**

**Presidential Primary Election Participation and Republican Percent of Total Primary Vote, 1972–1996**

| STATE | | 1972 | % | 1976 | % | 1980 | % | 1984 | % | 1988 | % | 1992 | % | 1996 | % |
|---|---|---|---|---|---|---|---|---|---|---|---|---|---|---|---|
| **Peripheral** | | | | | | | | | | | | | | | |
| Arkansas | Dem | ND | | ND | | 448,290 | | ND | | 97,544 | | 502,617 | | 300,389 | |
| | Rep | ND | 0% | ND | 0% | ND | 0% | ND | 0% | 68,305 | 41% | 52,141 | 9% | 42,814 | 13% |
| Florida | Dem | 1,264,554 | | 1,300,330 | | 1,182,003 | | 1,182,190 | | 1,273,298 | | 1,123,857 | | ND | |
| | Rep | 414,207 | 25% | 609,819 | 32% | 614,995 | 34% | 344,150 | 23% | 901,222 | 41% | 893,463 | 44% | 898,113 | 100% |
| N. Carolina | Dem | 821,405 | | 604,832 | | 737,262 | | 960,857 | | 679,958 | | 691,875 | | 572,160 | |
| | Rep | 167,899 | 17% | 193,727 | 24% | 168,391 | 19% | ND | 0% | 273,801 | 29% | 283,571 | 29% | 284,212 | 33% |
| Tennessee | Dem | ND | | 334,078 | | 294,680 | | 322,063 | | 576,314 | | 318,482 | | 137,797 | |
| | Rep | 114,489 | 100% | 242,535 | 42% | 195,210 | 40% | 82,921 | 21% | 254,252 | 31% | 254,653 | 44% | 289,386 | 68% |
| Texas | Dem | ND | | ND | | 1,377,354 | | ND | | 1,767,045 | | 1,482,975 | | 921,256 | |
| | Rep | ND | 0% | ND | 0% | 526,789 | 28% | 319,839 | 100% | 1,014,956 | 37% | 797,146 | 35% | 1,019,803 | 53% |
| Virginia | Dem | ND | | ND | | ND | | ND | | 364,899 | | ND | | ND | |
| | Rep | ND | 0% | ND | 0% | ND | 0% | ND | 0% | 234,142 | 39% | ND | 0% | ND | 0% |
| **Deep** | | | | | | | | | | | | | | | |
| Alabama | Dem | ND | | ND | | 237,464 | | 428,283 | | 405,642 | | 450,899 | | 302,030 | |
| | Rep | ND | 0% | ND | 0% | 211,353 | 47% | ND | 0% | 213,561 | 35% | 165,121 | 27% | 211,933 | 41% |
| Georgia | Dem | ND | | 502,471 | | 384,780 | | 684,541 | | 622,752 | | 454,631 | | 95,103 | |
| | Rep | ND | 0% | 188,472 | 27% | 200,171 | 34% | 50,793 | 7% | 400,928 | 39% | 453,990 | 50% | 559,067 | 86% |
| Louisiana | Dem | ND | | ND | | 358,741 | | 318,810 | | 642,450 | | 384,397 | | 154,701 | |
| | Rep | ND | 0% | ND | 0% | 41,683 | 10% | 16,687 | 5% | 144,781 | 18% | 135,109 | 26% | 77,789 | 34% |
| Mississippi | Dem | ND | | ND | | ND | | ND | | 359,417 | | 191,357 | | 93,788 | |
| | Rep | ND | 0% | ND | 0% | 25,751 | 100% | ND | 0% | 158,526 | 31% | 154,708 | 48% | 151,925 | 62% |
| S. Carolina | Dem | ND | | ND | | ND | | ND | | ND | | 116,414 | | ND | |
| | Rep | ND | 0% | ND | 0% | 145,501 | 100% | ND | 0% | 195,292 | 100% | 148,840 | 56% | 276,741 | 100% |

% = Republican; ND = No Data because there was either a party convention or no primary.

*Source:* Scammon, *America Votes*

president is running for re-election, the emergence of clear front-runners for open seats, and the comparative contest within each party's nomination process. Because eight of the eleven Southern states do not have party registration, voter registration lists are not very useful for comparing relative party strength in these states. In the absence of formal party registration, the resultant ability of voters to choose either party's primary is more open than in many parts of the country; for example, voters may vote in either party's primary on primary election day without having to register with the party at an earlier time. In addition, primaries typically do not engage the general electorate, but rather primarily draw the most active partisan identifiers (Nichols and Beck, 1995, p. 50). Thus, as Table 2.3 indicates, since 1988 it has become quite common in Southern states for increasing numbers of voters to participate in Republican presidential primaries. In 1996, when there was no contest for the Democratic nomination, more voters in six states—Florida, Tennessee, Texas, Georgia, Mississippi, and South Carolina—participated in the contested Republican primaries than in the Democratic primaries. In the three states that have party registration, Democrats continue to hold more formal registrants than Republicans (Florida—46.8 percent D, 41.5 percent R; Louisiana—65.4 percent D, 21.0 percent R; and North Carolina—56 percent D, 34 percent R), but at a presidential level Republicans still dominate general election outcomes in these states.

In the late 1800s and early 1900s it was a given that participation in the Democratic primary was essential to participate in politics in a meaningful way in the South because the legacy of the Civil War meant that only Democrats would be elected, and that being a Republican could mean loss of jobs, business contracts, or social connections and involvement. Now it is acceptable in the South to participate in the Republican primaries or to register as a Republican; and clearly, voting Republican has become the norm at the presidential level.

However, if one speaks of the growth of the Republican party as a political institution, or of changes in the pattern of voting and party realignment, it is necessary to look beyond the national, quadrennial election for president and to look at voting patterns for other national offices that are elected from within state boundaries and are influenced more by state and local issues and differences than one finds with presidential elections.

# *Chapter 3*

# The National Legislature

The United States Congress serves as a collection of state interests that come together to formulate the overall directions and substance of national policies. Although both the U.S. Senate and the U.S. House of Representatives are required to act as a whole to adopt legislation, they represent state and local interests to varying degrees. Because its members are elected statewide, the Senate brings a more broad-based set of state interests to the table, whereas the House members typically represent smaller districts that are more homogeneous and more susceptible to local issues and influences. House seats typically remain in one party's column for long periods of time, switching only when (1) boundaries have to be significantly redrawn, (2) the resident population experiences rapid racial or socio-economic change, (3) an individual with a particularly strong or compelling personality disrupts voting patterns, or (4) a serious scandal undoes an incumbent in the general elections rather than a party primary. Because of the differences, each congressional chamber will be examined separately.

## SOUTHERN SENATORS

A senator is elected statewide to a national office with responsibilities to bridge the gap between particular state concerns and na-

tional policies and goals. Whereas the South broke from its tradition
of voting for Democratic presidential candidates in 1948 by partially
defecting to a breakaway Democratic, third-party candidate, and to
a Republican candidate in 1952, GOP candidates for Senate had to
wait eight more years, or until 1960, before one of their members ran
successfully for a U.S. Senate seat in the South.

Table 3.1 presents the number of Republican seats won for the
U.S. Senate from 1960 to 1998. Of the possible races during this period in the six states composing the Peripheral South, GOP candidates contested 96 percent, while only 63 percent of the possible
contests in the five Deep South states were contested by Republican
candidates. Of the Deep South states, South Carolina was the only
state in which all senatorial races were contested after 1960. Only
Louisiana in the Deep South has resisted the Republican trend of
contesting elections; however, the unique election system in Louisiana where a candidate in the multi-party primary who captures 50
percent or more of the total vote is elected, has often resulted in a
Democratic candidate winning the Senate seat before the general
election, thus precluding a Republican challenge at that point.

For the first time, in 1990 incumbent Republican senators were
not contested by the Democrats in the Peripheral South state of Virginia and the Deep South state of Mississippi. That same year, incumbents David Pryor in Arkansas and Sam Nunn in Georgia were
the only Democratic candidates not challenged for re-election by a
Republican candidate. Beginning in 1994, all Senate seats in both
the Peripheral and Deep South have been contested.

Table 3.2 presents the percentage of the vote and the success of
Republican candidates for the U.S. Senate in Peripheral and Deep
South states. Senate contests in the South have been characterized
by ideological divisions between the Republican and Democratic
parties and within the Democratic party. During the 1960s and
1970s the majority of traditional White Southern Democrats were
strong supporters of military spending, economic development, racial segregation, and limited government, especially in social welfare programs. Liberal Southern Democrats were more likely to
support federal governmental intervention to improve race relations
and general social welfare for everyone. Similar divisions existed
within the Republican party, but the two groups were typically described as moderates and conservatives since few Republicans took
positions quite as liberal as some Democrats. The success of liberal,
moderate, or conservative candidates in either party's primary often

# Table 3.1
## Number of Republican U.S. Senate Seats and Contested Races, 1960–1998

| Year / State | 1960 | 1962 | 1964 | 1966 | 1968 | 1970 | 1972 | 1974 | 1976 | 1978 | 1980 | 1982 | 1984 | 1986 | 1988 | 1990 | 1992 | 1994 | 1996 | 1998 |
|---|---|---|---|---|---|---|---|---|---|---|---|---|---|---|---|---|---|---|---|---|
| **PERIPHERAL** | | | | | | | | | | | | | | | | | | | | |
| Arkansas | NRC | 0 | -- | NRC | 0 | -- | 0 | 0 | -- | 0 | 0 | -- | 0 | 0 | -- | NRC | 0 | -- | 1 | 0 |
| Florida | -- | 0 | 0 | -- | 1 | 0 | -- | 0 | 0 | -- | 1 | 0 | -- | 0 | 1 | -- | 0 | 1 | -- | 0 |
| N. Carolina | 0 | 0 | -- | 0 | 0 | -- | 1 | 0 | -- | 1 | 1 | -- | 1 | 0 | -- | 1 | 1 | -- | 1 | 0 |
| Tennessee | 0 | -- | 0/0* | 1 | -- | 1 | 1 | -- | 0 | 1 | -- | 0 | 0 | -- | 0 | 0 | -- | 1/1* | 1 | -- |
| Texas | 0 | 1* | 0 | 1 | -- | 0 | 1 | -- | 0 | 1 | -- | 0 | 1 | -- | 0 | 1 | -- | 1* | 1 | -- |
| Virginia | 0 | -- | 0 | 0/0* | -- | 0 | 1 | -- | NRC | 1 | -- | 1 | 1 | -- | 0 | 1 | -- | 0 | 1 | -- |
| Republican Wins | 0 | 1 | 0 | 2 | 1 | 1 | 4 | 0 | 0 | 4 | 2 | 1 | 3 | 0 | 1 | 3 | 1 | 4 | 5 | 0 |
| Total Contests | 5 | 4 | 5 | 6 | 3 | 4 | 5 | 3 | 4 | 5 | 3 | 4 | 5 | 3 | 4 | 5 | 3 | 5 | 5 | 4 |
| Total Periph. Rep. | 0 | 1 | 1 | 2 | 3 | 4 | 6 | 5 | 4 | 4 | 6 | 7 | 6 | 4 | 4 | 4 | 5 | 8 | 9 | 8 |
| **DEEP** | | | | | | | | | | | | | | | | | | | | |
| Alabama | 0 | 0 | -- | 0 | 0 | -- | 0 | NRC | -- | 0/0* | 1 | -- | 0 | 0 | -- | 0 | 0** | -- | 1 | 1 |
| Georgia | NRC | NRC | -- | NRC | 0 | -- | 0 | 0 | -- | 0 | 1 | -- | 0 | 0 | -- | NRC | 1 | -- | 0 | 1 |
| Louisiana | 0 | 0 | -- | NRC | NRC | -- | 0 | DP | -- | DP | DP | -- | DP | 0 | -- | DP | DP | -- | 0 | 0 |
| Mississippi | 0 | -- | NRC | 0 | -- | NRC | 0 | -- | NRC | 1 | -- | 0 | 1 | -- | 1 | NDC | -- | 1 | -- | -- |
| S. Carolina | NRC | 0 | -- | 1* | 0 | -- | 1 | 0 | -- | 1 | 0 | -- | 0 | 0 | -- | 1 | 0 | -- | 1 | 0 |
| Republican Wins | 0 | 0 | 0 | 1 | 0 | 0 | 1 | 0 | 0 | 2 | 2 | 0 | 2 | 0 | 1 | 2 | 1 | 1 | 3 | 2 |
| Total Contests | 5 | 4 | 1 | 5 | 4 | 1 | 5 | 4 | 1 | 6 | 4 | 1 | 5 | 4 | 1 | 5 | 4 | 1 | 5 | 4 |
| Total Deep Rep. | 0 | 0 | 0 | 1 | 1 | 1 | 1 | 1 | 1 | 2 | 4 | 4 | 4 | 2 | 3 | 3 | 5 | 5 | 6 | 6 |
| **SOUTH** | | | | | | | | | | | | | | | | | | | | |
| Republican Wins | 0 | 1 | 0 | 3 | 1 | 1 | 5 | 0 | 0 | 6 | 4 | 1 | 5 | 0 | 2 | 5 | 2 | 5 | 8 | 2 |
| TOTAL Rep. Seats | 0 | 1 | 1 | 3 | 4 | 5 | 7 | 6 | 5 | 6 | 10 | 11 | 10 | 6 | 7 | 7 | 9 | 13 | 15 | 14 |

NRC = No Republican Candidate; NDC = No Democratic; DP = Democrat Primary Win; *Special election; **Dem. won/switch to Rep.

**Table 3.2**
**Percentage of Republican Vote in General Elections for U.S. Senate, 1960–1998**

| YEAR | '60 | '62 | '64 | '66 | '68 | '70 | '72 | '74 | '76 | '78 | '80 | '82 | '84 | '86 | '88 | '90 | '92 | '94 | '96 | '98 |
|---|---|---|---|---|---|---|---|---|---|---|---|---|---|---|---|---|---|---|---|---|
| **STATE** | | | | | | | | | | | | | | | | | | | | |
| **PERIPHERAL** | | | | | | | | | | | | | | | | | | | | |
| Arkansas | NRC | 31 | | NRC | 41 | -- | 39 | 15 | -- | 16 | 41 | -- | 43 | 38 | -- | NRC | 40 | -- | 53* | 43 |
| Florida | | 30 | 36 | | 56* | 46 | -- | 41 | 37 | -- | 52* | 38 | -- | 45 | 50* | -- | 45 | 71* | -- | 37 |
| N. Carolina | 39 | 40 | | 44 | 39 | -- | 54* | 37 | -- | 55* | 50* | -- | 52* | 48 | -- | 53* | 50* | -- | 53* | 47 |
| Tennessee | 28 | | Sp47 46 | 56* | -- | 51* | 62* | -- | 47 | 56* | -- | 38 | 34 | -- | 35 | 30 | -- | 57* Sp61* | 61* | -- |
| Texas | 41 61Sp51* | | 44 | 56* | -- | 46 | 53* | -- | 42 | 50* | -- | 41 | 59* | -- | 40 | 60* | -- | 61* 93Sp67* | 55* | -- |
| Virginia | NRC | | 19 | 36 Sp37 | -- | 15 | 51* | -- | NRC | 50* | -- | 51* | 70* | -- | 29 | 100* | -- | 43 | 53* | -- |
| **DEEP** | | | | | | | | | | | | | | | | | | | | |
| Alabama | 30 | 49 | | 39 | 22 | -- | -- | NRC | -- | Sp43 Gn=NRC | 50* | -- | 36 | 50 | -- | 39 | 34** | -- | 53* | 63 |
| Georgia | NRC | NRC | | NRC | 23 | -- | 46 | 28 | -- | 17 | 51* | -- | 20 | 49 | -- | NRC | 48* | -- | 48 | 53 |
| Louisiana | 20 | 24 | | NRC | NRC | -- | 19 | DP | -- | DP | DP | -- | DP | 47 | -- | DP | DP | -- | 50 | 32 |
| Mississippi | 8 | | NRC | 27 | -- | NRC | 39 | -- | NRC | 45* | -- | 36 | 61* | -- | 54* | 100* | -- | 69* | 71* | -- |
| S. Carolina | NRC | 43 | | Sp49 62** | 38 | -- | 64* | 29 | -- | 56* | 30 | -- | 67* | 36 | -- | 64* | 47 | -- | 53* | 46 |

NRC = No Rep. Candidate; Sp = special election; Gn = general election; DP = Democrat primary win; * Rep. candidate won; ** Dem. won/switched to Rep.

*Sources: Guide to U.S. Elections; Scammon, America Votes*

influenced how segments of the party's voters would vote in the general election and thus which party's candidate would be elected.

Overall, Republican candidates have been much more successful in getting higher, respectable percentages of the vote and elected to the Senate in the Peripheral South than in the Deep South states. Republican candidates in the Deep South states had typically not been able to attract competitive percentages of the popular vote until the 1990s.

It was Texas, with no sizeable traditional Republican areas like other Peripheral states such as Tennessee, Virginia, and North Carolina, which became the first Southern state to send a Republican to the Senate in the twentieth century. John Tower narrowly won the special election in 1961 to fill Lyndon Johnson's Texas Senate seat when he was elected vice president in 1960. Tower won the election with considerable help from liberal Democrats who supported the national Democratic party, and crossed over to vote Republican, or "went fishin' "—stayed home and did not vote—in order to punish the traditional conservative wing of the state Democratic party, which had triumphed in the primary (Scher, 1997, p. 149). By 1966 Tower had established himself with a conservative Senate voting record that appealed to conservative Democrats and a firm hold on this first Republican Senate seat.

In 1966 Tower was joined by Howard Baker of Tennessee, who ran as a moderate/conservative. This early pattern of moderate/conservative to conservative Republicans being elected in both Peripheral and Deep South states has persisted to the present. Also elected in 1966 was Strom Thurmond of South Carolina, the former 1948 Dixiecrat/Democrat who switched to the GOP after Goldwater's 1964 candidacy. Both Baker and Thurmond were re-elected easily in 1972.

The march toward electing Republican senators in Peripheral South states continued when Florida added another Republican to the Senate in 1968, Edward Gurney, who defeated Leroy Collins by successfully labeling him a "liberal." Similarly, a second Tennessee Republican, Bill Brock, defeated the "liberal" Albert Gore, Sr., in 1970. In 1972, North Carolina's Jesse Helms, who switched to the Republican party just prior to the election, and Virginia's William Scott defeated moderate Democrats by successfully labeling their opponents as liberals, thus attracting numerous conservative Democratic voters.

By 1972, out of a total of twenty-two southern senators, seven were Republicans, but only one of the seven was from a Deep South state despite Goldwater's 1964 success in the Deep South at the presidential level (see Table 3.1). However, a successful strategy for Senate elections in the South was emerging. The pattern of fielding moderately conservative to very conservative Southern GOP Senate candidates, victorious over increasingly moderate to liberal Democratic candidates who were portrayed as very "liberal" and therefore either out of step with Southern voters, or worse, aligned with national Democratic policies set by Northerners and minority groups had triumphed, especially in the Peripheral South states.

It was also the case that during much of the 1960s and 1970s, one of Virginia's Senate seats was held by independent Harry Byrd, Jr. Although he tended to vote with the Democratic party in the Senate, it meant that from 1966 until 1981 Virginia did not officially elect a single Democrat to the Senate—the only state in the country with such a record. This could be viewed as a premonition of the pattern that was emerging in the South as allegiance to the Democratic party weakened, not just in Peripheral states, but in Deep South states as well.

In 1974 and 1976, in the wake of the Watergate scandal and Jimmy Carter's election to the presidency, Republicans failed to win a single Senate seat in the South. However, the GOP continued to maintain a success level of approximately one-third of the South's Senate seats during the 1970s. In the early Reagan years (1980 to 1984), Republicans held almost half of the Southern Senate seats, but could not sustain that level of success, dropping back to a third of the seats by 1986. Then in the 1994 election, Republicans claimed over half (59 percent or 13) of the 22 possible seats from Southern states, electing twelve GOP candidates and picking up a thirteenth seat—Richard Shelby in Alabama—through a party switch that followed his 1992 election as a Democrat. The Peripheral South states continued to be the stronger base for the GOP at this non-presidential level, capturing two-thirds of the Peripheral South Senate seats, whereas among Deep South states only half of the seats were held by the GOP. During this almost thirty-year time period, two Deep South states—Mississippi and South Carolina—accounted for most of the GOP success in this sub-region.

Nationally in 1996, thirty-four Senate seats were subject to election, and the Senate trend paralleled the presidential voting trends. The Democrats won 8 of the 12 Senate elections (66 percent) in the

East, Midwest, and Pacific regions of the country—the same regions Clinton carried overwhelmingly for the presidency. None of the four Republican winners received a majority of the votes cast. Republicans won 18 of 22 Senate seats (82 percent) in the so-called Republican "L"—the South, Plains, and Mountains. None of the four winning Democrats in these regions received more than 52 percent of the vote.

In 1996, the Republican pattern of success continued and increased in the South. Republicans held 75 percent of the Peripheral South Senate seats, including both seats in North Carolina, Tennessee, and Texas; and 60 percent of the seats in the Deep South, including both seats in Alabama and Mississippi. With the rapid disappearance of leading Democratic candidates in Arkansas as a result of political scandals that resulted in convictions in court and retirements, this previously weak Republican state elected Representative Tim Hutchinson to the Senate in 1996. Only Louisiana resisted the trend to elect Republicans to the Senate.

In 1998, the Republican and Democratic patterns held constant nationally. Of the thirty-four Senate seats to be elected in 1998, Republicans held 15 and the Democrats held 19 prior to the election. In the three regions carried by Clinton in 1996, 11 Democratic and 5 Republican seats were available, while in the three regions most supportive of Republican presidential candidates, the Republican "L," Republicans held 10 and the Democrats 8 seats. The total number of seats held nationally by each party overall and in the regional strongholds did not change after the 1998 election.

Partisan shifts did occur, however. In the East, Democrat Charles Schumer defeated incumbent Republican Alfonse D'Amato, solidifying the Democratic dominance in the Northeast. In the Midwest, which had been moving away from its traditional Republican alignment, Republican Peter Fitzgerald defeated incumbent Democrat Carol Moseley-Braun in Illinois, and former Republican Governor John Voinovich picked up the open seat vacated by retiring Democrat John Glenn. At the same time, in the most Republican state in the region, Indiana, former Democratic Governor Evan Bayh won the vacant seat of retiring Republican Daniel Coats. Across the river in Kentucky, in a very close race for the seat of retiring Democrat Wendell Ford, Republican Jim Bunning picked up the open seat.

In the South, Deep South Republican incumbents Richard Shelby in Alabama and Paul Coverdell in Georgia and Democratic incumbents Fritz Hollings in South Carolina and James Breaux in

Louisiana won re-election. In the Peripheral South, Democratic incumbent Bob Graham in Florida won re-election, and Democrat Blanche Lincoln held the open seat of retiring David Pryor in Arkansas, slowing a Republican trend in the state that witnessed Republican Senate and gubernatorial wins in 1996.

In a reversal of the Republican trend in the South generally, Democrat John Edwards defeated incumbent Republican Lauch Faircloth in North Carolina. No incumbent from either party has been re-elected in this Senate seat since the death of Democratic Senator John Ervin and the appointment of Robert Morgan to complete his unexpired term. Morgan was defeated in the next regular election in 1980 by Republican John East. When East committed suicide, Republican James Broyhill was appointed to complete East's term. In the 1986 election, former Democratic Governor Terry Sanford defeated Broyhill. After suffering a heart attack shortly before the election, Sanford was defeated in 1992 by Democrat-turned-Republican Lauch Faircloth. In 1998, newcomer, millionaire John Edwards defeated the incumbent, appealing to young voters, Faircloth's environmental record as a major hog farmer, and a general perception of a need for change. For the past eighteen years, the seat's party control has shifted—the only such record in the country—but this is also indicative of the partisan balance in this Peripheral South state.

Even with the net loss of one Republican seat in the South in 1998, Republicans still held 64 percent—14 of 22 Senate seats. Republicans held 75 percent of the seats in the Peripheral South and 60 percent of the seats in the Deep South, demonstrating a pervasive presence across the South as a region.

## SENATE PRIMARY PARTICIPATION

A further indicator of the strength of the Republican party in the South is the growth in voter participation in the Republican senatorial primaries (see Table 3.3). In general elections, voters are typically presented with two candidate choices—one Democrat and one Republican—and possible minor party candidates. Any registered voter can vote for any candidate on the ballot regardless of party. The most common way to influence who a party's candidate will be in the general election is to participate in the party's primary election. Party primaries allow those voters who identify with the political party to vote on the candidate who will represent the party in the

**Table 3.3**

**Total Votes Cast in Republican U.S. Senate Primaries in the South, 1972–1998**

| State/Year | '72 | '74 | '76 | '78 | '80 | '82 | '84 | '86 | '88 | '90 | '92 | '94 | '96 | '98 |
|---|---|---|---|---|---|---|---|---|---|---|---|---|---|---|
| **Peripheral** | | | | | | | | | | | | | | |
| Arkansas | unop | unop | ---- | unop | unop | ---- | unop | unop | ---- | NC | 52,238 | ---- | unop | 53,553 |
| Florida | ---- | 276,946 | 302,046 | ---- | 384,457 | 370,795 | ---- | 554,427 | 656,026 | ---- | 736,859 | unop | ---- | 550,188 |
| runoff | | | | | 476,511 | 226,662 | | | | | | | | |
| N. Carolina | 153,831 | 95,857 | ---- | unop | unop | ---- | 148,574 | 209,825 | ---- | 186,595 | 270,568 | ---- | unop | 259,836 |
| Tennessee | 249,954 | ---- | unop | 226,834 | ---- | 224,548 | 163,744 | ---- | 158,123 | 139,775 | ---- | 812,482* | 283,287 | ---- |
| Texas | unop | ---- | 356,307 | unop | ---- | 262,865 | 328,426 | ---- | 749,347 | unop | ---- | 555,338 | 986,202 | ---- |
| runoff | | | | | | | | | 184,707 | | | | | |
| Virginia | conv | ---- | conv | conv | ---- | conv | conv | ---- | conv | conv | ---- | unop | 493,535 | ---- |
| **Deep** | | | | | | | | | | | | | | |
| Alabama | 51,210 | conv | ---- | 21,578** | 115,533 | ---- | 43,186 | 33,659 | ---- | unop | 52,238 | ---- | 217,868 | unop |
| runoff | | | | | | | | | | | | | 137,753 | |
| Georgia | 78,418 | unop | ---- | 24,693 | 47,138 | ---- | 25,323 | 78,654 | ---- | NC | 269,943 | ---- | 446,655 | unop |
| runoff | | | | | | | | | | | 159,322 | | 320,800 | |
| Louisiana | 206,846 | NC | ---- | NC | 23,947 | ---- | 139,292 | 531,926 | ---- | 607,391 | 106,392 | ---- | 1.23M | 690,810 |
| runoff | | | | | | | | 646,311 | | | | | | |
| Mississippi | 23,228 | ---- | NC | 94,161 | ---- | 41,287 | unop | ---- | unop | unop | ---- | 76,019 | 145,575 | ---- |
| S. Carolina | unop | ---- | unop | 33,045 | ---- | 47,355 | 51,859 | ---- | unop | 160,924 | | ---- | 218,015 | 153,604 |
| runoff | | | | 10,570 | | | | | | | | | | |
| TOTAL | 556,641 | 372,803 | 658,353 | 367,266 | 604,120 | 899,495 | 895,900 | 1.46M | 1.56M | 347,855 | 1.65M | 1.44M | 4.48M | 1.7M |

conv = chosen by convention; unop = unopposed; NC = No candidate; *Combined full/short-term; **Special election.

*Sources: Guide to U.S. Elections; Scammon, America Votes*

general election against the other political party or parties. Most states across the country require that voters register their party preference prior to the primary election and then only those voters preferring the Republican party, for example, are allowed to vote in that party's primary election to determine the candidates to represent the party in the general election. In the South, only three states require party registration; therefore, voters may decide on the day of the primary election in which party's primary they wish to vote.

Voter participation in party primaries is typically no more than 25 percent of the registered voters. Voters are motivated to participate in a primary election if they think that their party's candidates have a chance to be elected in the general election. Voting for a candidate who stands no chance of getting elected is perceived by most voters as a waste of their time. Participation in a party's primary provides an indicator of voter perception of party viability in successfully electing its candidates to political office. Recognizing the particular circumstances in a given election and a given state, in every Southern state there is a general pattern of an increasing number of voters choosing to participate in the Republican party primaries for Senate.

Because of the overwhelming affiliation of African Americans with the Democratic party, virtually all of the Republican primary vote comes from White voters. In the wake of the 1965 Voting Rights Act, as the proportion of African American and Hispanic voters increased and their allegiance focused heavily on the Democratic party, Democratic senatorial candidates became more moderate to liberal on many social and political positions. As a result, more and more conservative White voters have begun to participate in the Republican primaries. This is a relatively new phenomenon because Republicans often did not have party primaries to select candidates when they were a small minority party, and because the absence of party registration allowed conservative Democrats to vote in the party primary of their choice without having to declare affiliation with a particular party.

An example of the obstacles to participation in Republican primaries in the past comes from the state of Arkansas. Until 1996 in Arkansas, primaries were financed by the political party from candidate filing fees allocated by a county election commission composed of a majority of the party controlling the state legislature. These officials allocated money for primary polling places. Because of the paucity of Republican candidates, few fees were available to finance the staffing of Republican polling places; hence, most people could not find a Republican polling place at which to vote, so the Democratic party primary remained the "only game" in town (Wekkin, 1997, p. 202).

The more moderate to liberal the Democratic candidates became as the percentage of the African American vote in the Democratic primary increased, the more conservative White voters opted for the Republican party. During the 1980s and 1990s most Democratic candidates for the Senate received 40 percent or less of the White vote and therefore had to receive overwhelming support from minority voters if they were to have a chance to win in the general election.

Every Southern state, especially in the 1990s, has witnessed an increase in the number of voters choosing to participate in the Republican primaries to select candidates for the party in U.S. Senate races. The presence of incumbent Republican senators in many of these races actually depresses the total Republican vote in that there is no reason to vote in the senatorial primary if there is no challenge within the party to the incumbent.

In 1998, thirty-four Senate seats were up for election nationally—18 Democratic seats and 16 Republican seats. Sixteen seats (11 Democrats and 5 Republicans) were in the East, Midwest, and Pacific regions that had tended toward Democratic preferences in the preceding two elections. Eighteen seats (7 Democrats and 11 Republicans) were in the South, Plains, and Mountains, regions that have more strongly supported Republican candidates in recent elections. In the South, 7 Senate seats were up for election. Of the 3 seats in Peripheral South states, 2 were held by Democrats and 1 by a Republican; and of the 4 Deep South seats, 2 were held by Democrats and 2 by Republicans.

After the 1998 election in the South, Democrats were able to pick up the Peripheral South seat of Lauch Faircloth in North Carolina, and to hold the other 4 Democratic seats in the South, including the open seat in Arkansas. Of the 18 Senate seats in the Republican "L," Republicans continued to hold the ten to eight advantage they had going into the election—losing the North Carolina seat, but picking up the open Democratic seat in Kentucky. In the other regions that have exhibited Democratic voting trends recently, the overall party breakdown remained unchanged even though 4 Senate seats switched party control—Democrats gaining seats in Indiana and New York, and Republicans gaining seats in Illinois and Ohio. The

1998 election confirmed a pattern of the parties' continued consolidation of their bases of geographic electoral strength.

Unlike two years earlier, two 1998 winning Republican candidates in the Republican "L" (the Plains, Mountains, and South) won with only 53 percent of the vote, while five of the eight winning Democratic candidates won with more than 55 percent of the vote, including three of the five victorious Democrats in the South. Incumbent Republican Coverdell in Georgia retained his seat with only 53 percent of the vote. In the more Democratic regions of the country—the East, Midwest, and Pacific—two of the five winning Republicans (Illinois and Kentucky) won with 51 percent or less of the vote, whereas only two of the eleven winning Democrats won with less than 55 percent of the votes cast. Since winning with 55 percent or more of the vote is considered to indicate a "safe" seat for the candidate, more balance between the parties surfaced in the 1998 midterm election. In the South, Republicans lost some ground, failing to pick up an open seat in Arkansas, and losing an incumbent seat in North Carolina.

The apparent trend in the South toward the Republican party waivered in 1998, but it is not clear whether this is a mild correction or another indication of Republican strength leveling off at a continuing competitive level with the Democratic party. Republican senatorial candidates, like their party's presidential candidates, now have a competitive position in virtually all Southern states.

## U.S. HOUSE OF REPRESENTATIVES

To gain a more detailed look at the impact of local issues on national legislative races, the vote for candidates for the U.S. House of Representatives can be totaled for a statewide figure. Paul T. David (*Party*, 1972, p. 16) found that House seats were closely linked to the vote for governor, which will be examined in more detail in the next chapter. The House figures are particularly useful to examine because they more readily reflect the local relationship of the representative to the district (i.e., "even though I don't like Congress very much, I like my representative"). Then, House races can be aggregated on a statewide basis to be used as an additional indicator of Republican strength within a state.

Southern states had always elected some Republicans to Congress, but following the Reconstruction period only Tennessee consistently continued to elect Republicans to the U.S. House. The

South as a region had a total of 106 seats in the House in 1968, increasing after each decennial census as the population of the region grew; by the 1992 election it had a total of 125 seats. Beginning in 1952, in addition to Tennessee's traditionally Republican 1st and 2nd Districts, the GOP won North Carolina's 10th District (Charlotte/Mecklenburg County) and Virginia's 10th (Alexandria), 6th (Roanoke), and 9th (which encompassed Virginia's traditionally Republican mountain voters). In 1954, Virginia's "Fighting Ninth" was lost, but Florida added the 1st District (Tampa-St. Petersburg) and Texas elected a Republican in the 5th (Dallas). Of these seven districts, two (the 1st and 2nd in Tennessee) were traditional Mountain Republican districts, two combined a "mountain" vote with a larger urban vote (Virginia's 6th and North Carolina's 10th), and three were urban districts (Virginia's 10th, Florida's 1st, and Texas' 5th). The two bases of Republicanism in the South—historic mountain areas that had opposed secession at the time of the Civil War and growing urban areas—had begun to exhibit Republican success in winning U.S. House elections.

   The Republican party continued to hold the seven districts it won in 1954 until 1962 when Florida added a second urban GOP seat, North Carolina added a "mountain" district, and Tennessee added the 3rd District (Chattanooga and "Mountain"). The Goldwater candidacy in 1964 did not appreciably affect the number of Republican House seats in the Peripheral South states (although the Dallas seat was lost); however, the Deep South states responded by electing seven Republican House members. Of the five seats contested by the GOP in Alabama, the 1st (Mobile), 2nd (Montgomery), 4th and 6th (Black Belt districts), and the 7th (upcountry, including the "Free State of Winston") Districts all elected Republicans. Alabama's Winston County had resisted secession at the time of the Civil War and had tried unsuccessfully to secede from the state at the time. Georgia elected a Republican in the 3rd District (Columbus/Black Belt), and Mississippi placed the 4th District (Jackson/Vicksburg/Black Belt) in the GOP column.

   The Goldwater candidacy did not help GOP candidates in the Peripheral South, and if the Dallas seat that was lost was an indication, Goldwater may have cost Republican gains outside the Deep South. Bernard Cosman (*Five States*, 1967, p. 90) claims that Goldwater's candidacy polarized the Deep South vote around race, attracting White votes in Black Belt areas, but losing White urban votes in areas that had supported the Republican party in past elections. "At the Southwide level, the Goldwater candidacy brought about an apparent reversal of very long-standing, presidential voting alignments . . . [by doing] best in black-belt, least well in the cities. There is no precedent anywhere in the electoral data of the last four decades for either the arrangement of the Goldwater percentages by sector or the emergence of black-belt presidential Republicanism on such a grand scale . . . The Goldwater outcome in the Deep South more nearly fits the traditional mold of southern political behavior than it fits the alignment of the 1952–60 period" (Cosman, *Five States*, 1967, pp. 51–52; 90–91).

Table 3.4 indicates the changes in voting patterns among four voter sub-groups within the Southern population and the effect that Goldwater's candidacy had on Southern voters. As Cosman suggests in his book, *Five States for Goldwater*, the Old Confederacy gave Goldwater 271 of its 278 Republican convention votes at the 1964 Republican nominating convention and was determined to work for his election and the election of his running mates at the local levels (Cosman, *Five States*, 1967, p. 16). In the Deep South, Goldwater increased Republican votes among each of the four voter groups, especially rural, non-metropolitan and Black-Belt voters who were primarily White and traditionally Democratic. Peripheral South voters were less enthusiastic, except in Black-Belt regions where White Democrats provided a larger Republican vote at the presidential level than in the previous election.

**Table 3.4**
**Presidential Republican Vote Gain/Loss, 1960–1964**

| Voter Group | Percentage Gain/Loss, 1960-1964 | |
|---|---|---|
| | DEEP SOUTH | PERIPHERAL SOUTH |
| Traditional Mountain | 7.6 | -9.3 |
| Metropolitan | 15.8 | -8.4 |
| Rural, Non-metropolitan | 30.9 | -8.5 |
| Black-Belt | 40.4 | 10.6 |

*Source*: Cosman, *Five States for Goldwater*, 1967, pp. 56, 61, 95

According to Cosman, "Deep South Republican leaders of today, unlike their counterparts of yesteryear, were out to alter the political landscape of their subregion" (Cosman, *Five States*, 1967, p. 16). And they did at the presidential level, as well as at the more "local" level, electing seven House members and numerous city and county officials in Alabama, South Carolina, and Mississippi. Goldwater had broken the Deep South's monolithic rejection of the Republican party at the non-presidential level that had persisted even through the 1948 split in the Democratic party and the popular candidacy of Eisenhower in the 1950s. The breakthrough, however, was not fully realized until more recently.

By 1966 many voters were returning to their pre-1964 patterns. Three of Alabama's five Republican House seats were lost. The GOP retained the newly reapportioned 1st (Mobile) and 2nd (Montgomery) Districts, and won the new 6th (Birmingham) District. The pattern that Donald Strong found of increasing Republican voting tendencies among urban voters and higher income voters began to reassert itself as Black Belt Republicanism dropped (Strong, *1952 Presidential*, 1953).

Arkansas, as a result of reapportioned districts in 1966, finally managed to combine its traditional Mountain Republican strength with a slowly growing urban GOP base in Ft. Smith and Hot Springs to capture the 3rd District seat. Florida, reapportioned in 1965, added the Ft. Lauderdale district to its two previous Republican victories in Tampa/St. Petersburg and Orlando. In a stunning change from the past, the 5th District (Orlando) GOP candidate ran unopposed!

Georgia rather dramatically demonstrated the reversion to an urban-based Republicanism in 1966 by returning the rural 3rd District to the Democrats, but capturing the 4th and 5th Districts in and around Atlanta. Louisiana held firmly to the Democratic tradition, and the lone Republican congressman in Mississippi lost his seat. South Carolina, though, provided another GOP gain, as former Goldwater-Democrat Albert Watson was re-elected in the 2nd (Columbia) District as a Republican.

In the Peripheral South, North Carolina added a GOP victory in the 4th District (Raleigh) to the two seats already held. Tennessee added a fourth seat, the 9th District (Memphis). Texas sent two congressmen to the House from the 7th (Houston) and the 18th (Amarillo) Districts. Virginia recorded two more GOP House members in the 8th and 9th Districts for a total of 23 Southern Republican members of the House in 1966.

The three Republicans in Alabama's metropolitan districts (the 1st, 2nd, and 6th) were returned to Washington through the 1972 elections, as was the lone GOP congressman from Arkansas. Florida had four GOP congressmen after the 1972 reapportionment and election—the 6th (Tampa/St. Petersburg), 9th (Orlando), 10th (Ft. Myers, West Palm Beach, and South Central Florida), and the 12th (Ft. Lauderdale, Hollywood).

The election of 1972 saw the first Republican congressman from Louisiana since Reconstruction who was elected in the 3rd District (New Orleans suburbs). Mississippi elected Republicans for the first time since 1964 in the 4th (Jackson, Vicksburg) and the 5th (Gulfport, Biloxi) Districts.

North Carolina, redistricted in 1971, had four GOP members from the new 8th, 9th (Charlotte), 10th (Mountain), and 5th (Winston-Salem and Mountain) Districts. In 1972, South Carolina added the 6th District to its GOP control of the 2nd (Columbia). Tennessee added a fourth GOP seat in 1972, the 6th District (Memphis suburbs, West Central Tennessee).

Texas had three GOP seats in 1968, the 7th, the 18th, and the 3rd (Dallas) Districts, and by 1972 had increased the total to four—the 3rd and 5th (Dallas), the 7th (Houston), and the 13th (Amarillo and the Panhandle). Virginia had the steadiest increase in GOP seats. To the four seats held in 1966 (the 6th, 8th, 9th, and 10th), the 2nd (Norfolk) was added in 1968, the 7th (Northwest Virginia) in 1970, and the 4th (Portsmouth) in 1972. Georgia in 1972 was the only Southern state to have a net loss of a seat in the House. Andrew Young captured the redistricted 5th, leaving the Republicans with only the 4th (DeKalb and Rockdale Counties) District.

By the time of the 1972 Nixon re-election sweep for the new Republican Solid South at the presidential level, of the 34 GOP House seats out of the 107 allocated to the South, 25 came from the six Peripheral South states and the remaining 9 came from the five Deep South states. Of the 34 GOP districts held, 17 were urban or suburban districts, 5 were heavily urban, 3 combined urban votes with traditional Republican Mountain strength, 7 were in traditional Republican areas, and 2 districts were predominantly non-metropolitan districts.

The trends that Donald Strong found as far back as 1940–1944 of a rising urban Republicanism were very evident in the South by the time Burnham (1991) suggested that politically the United States had moved into a post-Industrial/post-Party political era wherein party was not as important as the candidate. As was the case in the rest of the country, it was among the higher income, suburban dwellers that Republican voting manifested itself most strongly in the Peripheral South. And although it had greatly receded by 1966, the force of the Goldwater candidacy in 1964 was still visible in both the Deep South and Peripheral South states. In Mississippi's 4th District urban Republicans and Black Belt Whites united in the face of a 43 percent Black population to elect a Republican, and the voters of the 5th District elected the Democrat-turned-Republican administrative assistant of the venerable Democratic Congressman Colmer upon the latter's retirement in 1972. In Alabama urban voters and some Black Belt Whites aligned to keep the 1st and 2nd Districts safely Republican. And in South Carolina urban and Black Belt Whites joined together to elect Republicans in the face of a perceived threat that a 34 percent Black population in the 2nd District (Columbia) and a 42 percent Black population in the 6th District might elect a Black candidate. Although race remains an issue in the Deep South, as these states become more urbanized and industrialized, the power of the race issue may give way to class differentials and cleavages similar to those in the rest of the nation, including the Peripheral South.

Tracing the pattern of Republican success in U.S. House races since 1968—the election that began to reflect the involvement of an increased proportion of the African American population after the implementation of the 1965 Voting Rights Act—Republican totals in the South hovered around one-fourth to one-third of the available seats throughout the 1970s and 1980s (see Table 3.5). The Republican success continued the pattern established in the 1950s by electing candidates in primarily traditional Republican areas (dating from the time of the Civil War) and from primarily urban/suburban areas populated by middle-class professionals, in-migrants from other parts of the country who brought their Republicanism with them, and older individuals retiring to warmer climates. Conservative White Democrats continued to represent many rural districts across the South.

Even though two states—Tennessee and Virginia—actually sent a Republican majority of their U.S. House delegations to Congress as early as 1970/72, it was not sustained in succeeding elections with any reliability. By 1998 only three states in the South—Texas, Vir-

## Table 3.5
## Number of Republican U.S. House Seats Won in the South, 1968–1998

| State/Year | '68 | '70 | '72 | '74 | '76 | '78 | '80 | '82 | '84 | '86 | '88 | '90 | '92 | '94 | '96 | '98 | TOTAL |
|---|---|---|---|---|---|---|---|---|---|---|---|---|---|---|---|---|---|
| **Peripheral** | | | | | | | | | | | | | | | | | |
| Arkansas | 1/4 | 1/4 | 1/4 | 1/4 | 1/4 | 2/4 | 2/4 | 2/4 | 1/4 | 1/4 | 1/4 | 1/4 | 2/4 | 2/4 | 2/4 | 2/4 | 23/64 |
| Florida | 3/12 | 3/12 | 4/15 | 5/15 | 5/15 | 3/15 | 4/15 | 6/19 | 7/19 | 8/19 | 9/19 | 10/19 | 13/23 | 15/23 | 15/23 | 15/23 | 125/286 |
| N. Carolina | 4/11 | 4/11 | 4/11 | 2/11 | 2/11 | 2/11 | 3/11 | 2/11 | 5/11 | 3/11 | 3/11 | 4/11 | 4/12 | 8/12 | 6/12 | 7/12 | 63/180 |
| Tennessee | 4/9 | 4/9 | 5/9 | 3/8 | 3/8 | 3/8 | 3/8 | 3/9 | 3/9 | 3/9 | 3/9 | 3/9 | 4/9 | 5/9 | 5/9 | 5/9 | 59/140 |
| Texas | 3/23 | 3/23 | 4/23 | 3/24 | 3/24 | 4/24 | 5/24 | 5/27 | 9/27 | 10/27 | 8/27 | 8/27 | 9/30 | 11/30 | 13/30 | 13/30 | 111/420 |
| Virginia | 5/10 | 6/10 | 7/10 | 5/10 | 6/10 | 6/10 | 8/10 | 5/10 | 5/10 | 5/10 | 5/10 | 4/10 | 4/11 | 5/11 | 5/11 | 5/11 | 86/164 |
| **Deep** | | | | | | | | | | | | | | | | | |
| Alabama | 3/8 | 3/8 | 3/7 | 3/7 | 3/7 | 3/7 | 2/7 | 2/7 | 2/7 | 2/7 | 2/7 | 3/7 | 3/7 | 3/7 | 5/7 | 5/7 | 47/114 |
| Georgia | 2/10 | 2/10 | 1/10 | 0/10 | 0/10 | 1/10 | 1/10 | 1/10 | 2/10 | 2/10 | 1/10 | 1/10 | 4/11 | 7/11 | 8/11 | 8/11 | 41/164 |
| Louisiana | 0/8 | 0/8 | 1/8 | 2/8 | 2/8 | 3/8 | 2/8 | 2/8 | 2/8 | 3/8 | 4/8 | 4/8 | 3/7 | 3/7 | 5/7 | 5/7 | 41/124 |
| Mississippi | 0/5 | 0/5 | 2/5 | 2/5 | 2/5 | 2/5 | 2/5 | 2/5 | 2/5 | 1/5 | 1/5 | 0/5 | 0/5 | 1/5 | 3/5 | 2/5 | 22/80 |
| S. Carolina | 1/6 | 1/6 | 2/6 | 1/6 | 1/6 | 2/6 | 4/6 | 3/6 | 3/6 | 2/6 | 2/6 | 2/6 | 3/6 | 4/6 | 4/6 | 4/6 | 39/96 |
| Total Rep. | 26 | 27 | 34 | 27 | 28 | 31 | 36 | 33 | 41 | 40 | 39 | 40 | 49 | 64 | 71 | 71 | |
| Total Seats | 106 | 106 | 107 | 107 | 108 | 108 | 108 | 116 | 116 | 116 | 116 | 116 | 125 | 125 | 125 | 125 | |
| % Rep. | 24.53 | 25.47 | 31.78 | 25.23 | 26.42 | 29.24 | 33.96 | 28.94 | 35.96 | 35.09 | 34.21 | 35.08 | 40.16 | 52.03 | 56.8 | 56.8 | |

*Sources: Guide to U.S. Elections; Scammon, America Votes*

ginia, and Mississippi—did *not* send a majority Republican delegation to the U.S. House. The 1994 Republican Revolution year,
followed by 1996 in the South, seemed to solidify a Republican majority in the South's House delegations.

Because the majority party in state legislatures determines the
boundaries of congressional districts and typically tries to concentrate the voters of the opposition party into as few districts as possible in order to elect as many members of their own party as they can
in the remaining districts, the percentage of the votes cast by voters
for each major party is another indicator of the strength of the party
in a state at the congressional level. Although Tennessee has had
the longest history of sending Republican House members to Congress, Virginia was the earliest to send a majority of its statewide total House delegation to Congress composed of Republican
members.

In the Republican Revolution year of 1994, every Southern state
except Mississippi and Louisiana cast 50 percent of its House votes
for Republican candidates (see Table 3.6). The percentage of the
votes cast for Republican candidates in the general election does not
necessarily coincide perfectly with the number of House seats won
by the party. For example, in 1994 Mississippi elected only one of
five House members, or 20 percent of the seats, while casting 42
percent of its votes for Republican candidates. Republican voters in
1994 were under-represented in the U.S. House. By 1996 this situation had changed considerably—Mississippi cast almost 54 percent
of its House votes for Republican candidates, electing three of five
House members or 60 percent. In 1996, Deep South states in particular parlayed 50–60 percent of the House votes into 60–70 percent of the House seats in their states, although the percentage of
the House seats in Peripheral South states (52 percent) more closely
corresponded to the percentage of House votes (48 percent) statewide for Republican candidates. The 1998 election witnessed little
change from the 1996 electoral pattern in the South.

Texas is the state in which the number of Republican seats in its
U.S. House delegation has lagged furthest behind its total U.S.
House votes; that is, while 50 percent of its House votes have gone to
Republican candidates in recent elections, approximately 40 per-
cent of the seats have been won by Republicans. On the other hand,
Georgia is the most egregious example of over-representation based
on percentage of Republican House votes, casting slightly over half
of its House votes for Republicans and electing nearly three-fourths

**Table 3.6**

**Average Percentage of Republican Vote in General Elections for U.S. House, 1968-1998**

| YEAR | 1968 | 1970 | 1972 | 1974 | 1976 | 1978 | 1980 | 1982 | 1984 | 1986 | 1988 | 1990 | 1992 | 1994 | 1996 | 1998 |
|---|---|---|---|---|---|---|---|---|---|---|---|---|---|---|---|---|
| **STATE** | | | | | | | | | | | | | | | | |
| **Peripheral** | | | | | | | | | | | | | | | | |
| Arkansas | 53 | 67 | 77 | 37 | 22 | 67 | 79 | 48 | 19 | 41 | 42 | 44 | 40 | 53 | 53 | 45 |
| Florida | 43 | 46 | 47 | 55 | 45 | 39 | 46 | 41 | 53 | 49 | 53 | 52 | 53 | 50 | 32 | 65 |
| N. Carolina | 45 | 44 | 45 | 35 | 35 | 40 | 44 | 45 | 39 | 43 | 44 | 46 | 48 | 54 | 53 | 54 |
| Tennessee | 50 | 41 | 53 | 40 | 31 | 42 | 47 | 38 | 45 | 41 | 37 | 40 | 45 | 55 | 50 | 50 |
| Texas | 28 | 26 | 29 | 27 | 35 | 48 | 41 | 33 | 55 | 43 | 40 | 51 | 50 | 53 | 50 | 47 |
| Virginia | 44 | 46 | 46 | 39 | 46 | 56 | 66 | 53 | 56 | 43 | 54 | 36 | 49 | 54 | 51 | 41 |
| **Deep** | | | | | | | | | | | | | | | | |
| Alabama | 27 | 26 | 39 | 30 | 32 | 31 | 34 | 33 | 28 | 26 | 39 | 31 | 42 | 56 | 53 | 55 |
| Georgia | 21 | 26 | 28 | 28 | 25 | 20 | 28 | 37 | 26 | 28 | 27 | 33 | 45 | 57 | 51 | 56 |
| Louisiana | 19 | 6 | 13 | 26 | 28 | 37 | 33 | 28 | 37 | 24 | 44 | 35 | 49 | 49 | 29 60%** | 31.3 |
| Mississippi | 8 | 9 | 22 | 43 | 40 | 46 | 39 | 41 | 26 | 47 | 34 | 19 | 28 | 42 | 54 | 43 |
| S. Carolina | 32 | 27 | 48 | 41 | 36 | 32 | 48 | 45 | 48 | 37 | 44 | 41 | 52 | 57 | 65 | 62 |

**Percent Republican vote in primary, Florida permitted tallying of unopposed votes after 1986—not required.
*Source:* Data derived from Scammon, *America Votes*

of its House members. Clearly, districting and turnout have had a large impact on House elections. Whereas in the past Republicans were consistently under-represented based on their actual numbers in the electorate, by 1996 they had reached parity or even over-representation in much of the South. In the 1996 election, the South as a region was the only region to cast a majority of its House votes for Republican candidates (Cook, "Thinnest of Margins," 1997, p. 441). The 1998 election exhibited continuity overall in the South in both the number of seats won by Republicans (71 total)—Republicans lost a seat in Mississippi, but gained a seat in North Carolina—and the percentage of congressional votes cast for Republican candidates.

Another indicator of the convergence of the Deep South and the Peripheral South, as well as increasing similarity with the remainder of the country, is reflected in the pattern of Republican voting for the House. Both the Deep South and the Peripheral South states have moved into the national pattern of increased numbers of voters in a presidential election and substantial decreases in the number of voters in off-year elections. Table 3.7 also suggests that the core Republican vote in the Deep South is firmer than in the Peripheral South—there is much less variation between the Republican vote for House candidates in presidential years and in off-year elections in Deep South states than in Peripheral South states. Peripheral South states exhibit a one to one-and-a-half million vote decrease for House candidates in off-year elections compared to presidential years, while Deep South states witness only a half-million to one-million vote decline. House races appear to have a higher salience for Deep South voters, or the Deep South Republican voters are more persistent in their Republican voting behavior.

The inability of Bob Dole in 1996 to draw Republican voters to the polls and its potential impact at the level of House elections is reflected in the extremely small increase in Republican vote for House members in Peripheral South states, whereas a typical increase in Republican voting appears in the Deep South states—excluding Louisiana with its system of deciding most elections in the primary. In 1996 there was no net gain of House seats in Peripheral South states with an increase in total Republican vote for House seats of just under 200,000 votes; while in Deep South states, Republicans gained 7 seats over their 1994 total in the House and saw a Republican vote increase of almost 1.2 million votes. The falloff in the typical

# Table 3.7
## Number of Republican Votes Cast in General Elections for U.S. House, 1972–1998

| State/Year | '72* | '74 | '76* | '78 | '80* | '82 | '84* | '86 | '88* | '90 | '92* | '94 | '96* | '98 |
|---|---|---|---|---|---|---|---|---|---|---|---|---|---|---|
| **Peripheral** | | | | | | | | | | | | | | |
| Arkansas | 144,571 | 156,183 | 75,384 | 195,371 | 159,148 | 360,983 | 86,632 | 264,777 | 250,268 | 295,877 | 354,553 | 371,556 | 456,033 | 319,534 |
| Florida | 900,683 | 580,975 | 937,257 | 634,045 | 1.43M | 899,110 | 1.09M | 805,754 | 1.59M | 1.16M | 2.48M | 1.02M | 1.49M | 556,939 |
| N. Carolina | 609,926 | 347,603 | 549,410 | 406,076 | 769,144 | 578,893 | 830,844 | 679,981 | 784,908 | 935,054 | 1.18M | 804,416 | 1.34M | 992,476 |
| Tennessee | 589,272 | 363,502 | 389,058 | 448,825 | 618,876 | 361,899 | 587,604 | 450,309 | 534,429 | 288,633 | 739,371 | 770,424 | 88,546 | 377,845 |
| Texas | 835,185 | 406,744 | 1.28M | 1.05M | 1.60M | 852,907 | 1.92M | 1.21M | 1.81M | 1.50M | 2.60M | 2.05M | 1.64M | 1.77M |
| Virginia | 589,573 | 361,302 | 607,400 | 594,915 | 995,892 | 689,620 | 1.01M | 462,975 | 941,347 | 410,941 | 1.13M | 947,705 | 1.12M | 521,838 |
| TOTAL: | 3.67M | 2.22M | 3.84M | 3.33M | 5.58M | 3.74M | 5.53M | 3.87M | 5.91M | 4.59M | 8.49M | 5.96M | 6.13M | 4.53M |
| **Deep** | | | | | | | | | | | | | | |
| Alabama | 383,623 | 169,304 | 314,970 | 197,176 | 354,224 | 265,842 | 285,074 | 424,527 | 418,467 | 314,735 | 639,426 | 554,310 | 785,513 | 541,407 |
| Georgia | 252,901 | 230,769 | 310,062 | 116,301 | 381,174 | 199,941 | 422,319 | 286,479 | 552,429 | 538,865 | 991,556 | 808,325 | 1.12M | 701,403 |
| Louisiana** | 86,607 | 140,008 | 289,008 | 277,763 | 253,654 | 142,371 | 238,794 | 187,329 | 269,776 | 351,516 | 547,551 | ND | 135,990 | 96,944 |
| Mississippi | 224,067 | 130,999 | 256,608 | 236,274 | 304,472 | 258,152 | 181,147 | 206,187 | 303,808 | 69,216 | 266,969 | 252,120 | 487,988 | 227,185 |
| S. Carolina | 301,527 | 212,893 | 279,390 | 183,369 | 399,039 | 293,062 | 402,760 | 261,435 | 434,730 | 274,650 | 577,052 | 418,091 | 682,563 | 573,342 |
| TOTAL: | 1.25M* | 883,973 | 1.45M* | 1.01M | 1.69M* | 1.16M | 1.53M* | 1.37M | 1.98M* | 1.55M | 3.03M* | 2.03M | 3.21M* | 2.14M |

*Presidential Election Year; **Votes not tallied for unopposed candidates; ND = No Data Reported.

Sources: Scammon, America Votes; Guide to U.S. Elections

Republican increase in voting may well have cost Republican gains in House seats in Peripheral South states.

## REDISTRICTING AND HOUSE ELECTIONS

In the 1990s the whirlwind of political change hit the South with a vengeance. The 1990 Census added 4 House seats to Florida; 3 seats to Texas; 1 each to North Carolina,Virginia, and Georgia; and Louisiana lost 1 seat. Redistricting resulted in a surge of Republicans elected to the House, Democratic retirements, and party switching by Democrats to the Republican party. By 1998, Republicans held almost 57 percent of the House seats from the South. The strongest breakthroughs were among the Deep South states where 67 percent of the seats were held by Republicans compared to 53 percent in the Peripheral states. By 1998, Republican representatives constituted a majority in four of five Deep South state delegations, whereas they were a majority in only three of six Peripheral South state delegations to Congress. Arkansas' congressional delegation remained tied with 2 Republican representatives and 2 Democratic representatives.

As primarily Democratic state legislatures scrambled to redistrict House seats in the 1990s, the U.S. Supreme Court and the U.S. Department of Justice (DOJ) further complicated the electoral process. Section 5 of the 1965 Voting Rights Act was designed to keep Southern states (except Tennessee and Arkansas, which are not covered by the Voting Rights Act (VRA) because they had not adopted legislation prohibiting Black political participation) from erecting further barriers to minority participation and representation. The 1982 amendments to the VRA clearly recognized African Americans as a protected class, expanded the application of the VRA to the nation as a whole (not just the South), and established a standard for violation of the act that examined the "totality of the circumstances." A violation could be considered to have occurred if African Americans could not participate equally with the majority in the political process and elect their own candidates to public office. The Department of Justice interpreted these provisions to mean that states had to maximize election districts for the House and the state legislatures so that they would have a majority of minority voters in the districts.

The federal courts also appeared to support this interpretation in such cases as *Thornburg v. Gingles* (1986) wherein multi-member districts were struck down as violative of the VRA. The result was that most states in the South drew new districts that concentrated African American and Hispanic voters into a few majority-minority districts. By the 1990s minority voters were a mainstay of Democratic electoral success, which resulted in majority-majority districts becoming increasingly susceptible to Republican capture because by this time in no Southern state was a majority of the White voters supporting Democratic candidates.

In some states such as Georgia and North Carolina, legislative maps bounced back and forth between state capitals and the Department of Justice as the Department insisted on more majority-minority districts. Some of these redrawn districts closely resembled the famous reptilian electoral districts of Governor Gerry of Massachusetts a century earlier that resulted in coining the term "gerrymandering" to describe oddly shaped districts drawn to place most members of an identifiable voter group into a single district. These gerrymandered districts thus ensured the election of a candidate favored by that group but diminished the group's ability to influence the election of candidates they favored in surrounding districts. As Lublin found, "racial redistricting alters not only the aggregation of votes but also the quality of candidates presented, such that it indirectly boosts the Republican share of votes and seats by undercutting Democratic prospects . . . in districts surrounding majority-minority districts in the South" (1999, p.186).

Another result of the efforts to redistrict in order to create majority-minority districts was the creation of more safe districts for the two major political parties. In 1998 in the South, 51 percent, or 36 of the 71 House Republicans elected, were unopposed by a Democratic candidate. At the same time, 44 percent, or 23 of the 52 Democrats elected, had no Republican opposition in the general election. Forty-seven percent of the House members from the South did not have major party opposition and in most instances had no opposition at all in the general election in 1998.

Once approved by the Department of Justice, the new districts for U.S. House members and state legislators resulted in the election of more African American and Hispanic representatives. In addition, they resulted in a steep decline in the number of White Democrats in the House as the absence (or at least large decrease in the number) of minority Democratic votes in some districts was accompanied by the increasing tendency of White voters to support conservative Republican candidates. In the Deep South, for example, only eleven Democrats were elected to the House in 1996. Of those eleven, seven were African American and four were White. All of the Republicans were White.

In 1990, there were only six House districts in the South with more than 40 percent African American population. In 1996 there were fifteen such districts. None of the eleven districts with a majority African American population elected Republicans, whereas one of the four districts with 40–49.9 percent African American population elected a Republican representative. Since African Americans vote overwhelmingly Democratic, it means that virtually all White voters in these districts were voting Republican. In 1990, only 36 House districts had less than 10 percent African American population; in 1996 the number increased to 51 districts. Over 78 percent of the districts with less than 10 percent minority population were represented by Republicans (Bullock and Rozell, 1998, p. 14). It is estimated that between 12 to 20 House districts became Republican due to the creation of the 11 majority-minority districts in the early 1990s (Scher, 1997, p. 150). Lublin further argued that the loss of White Democratic members also resulted in the House's failure to adopt initiatives supported by Blacks (1999, p. 185).

Race remains an important factor in the electoral politics of the South. Whereas in the earlier part of the twentieth century the Southern Democratic party stood firmly on the color line, the transformation of the Democratic party has altered the Southern landscape. During most of the 1900s the Republican party was unable to "beat" the Democrats in most elections, so they pursued a strategy of adopting many of the traditional Southern Democratic positions on social and economic issues. If you cannot "beat" them, then "join" them. The Southern Strategy of the Nixon/Reagan years—selecting candidates and issues that appealed to White rural and conservative voters—has finally blossomed and borne fruit.

The dedication of the Department of Justice to increase minority representation has had the effect of decimating White Democratic candidates in the South. In the wake of this political transformation in the early 1990s, the federal courts by 1993 began to forcefully limit the Department of Justice by declaring some gerrymandered majority-minority districts unconstitutional. In *Shaw v. Reno* (1993) the Supreme Court questioned the shape of the 12th District in North Carolina that had been created to form a second majority-minority district in the state, but did not rule on the merits of the case. Also in 1993, a federal district court ruled the 4th congressional District in Louisiana and the legislative act that created it unconstitutional in *Hays v. Louisiana* (1993). In *Miller v. Johnson* (115 S. Ct. 2475 [1995]), the Supreme Court struck down the 11th District in Georgia because it violated the Equal Protection clause, having been drawn primarily on the basis of race. Later, Georgia's 2nd District was also declared unconstitutional. In *Shaw v. Hunt* (1998), the federal courts finally struck down North Carolina's 12th District for similar reasons and ordered new districts to be drawn. *Miller* concluded that race can be one criterion under the Supreme Court's strict scrutiny rule, but race cannot be the "overriding and predominant force" driving the districting process.

With White Democrats still in control of both the Georgia and the North Carolina legislatures, the realization that Democratic chances for election in both U.S. House and state legislative elections might be enhanced by moving more minority voters into White majority districts may yet occur. Under current court orders majority-minority districts must become more compact (*Shaw v. Hunt*), which may make it harder to maintain their minority majority but not necessarily their Democratic majority. Indeed, in the 1998 election the redrawn 12th District of North Carolina lost its African American majority but not its Democratic majority. Mel Watt, the African American first elected when the district was a majority-minority district, was re-elected with 56 percent of the vote in 1998. Similarly, Cynthia McKinney and Sanford Bishop in Georgia, first elected in majority-minority districts, were re-elected in redrawn majority White districts with well over 50 percent of the votes in 1998.

Brady, Cogan, and Rivers (1997) observed that the late 1990s were a time when the conditions associated with GOP success—Democrats representing small concentrations of African Americans and Democratic legislators with voting records too liberal for their districts—were most common. Republican gains in the House may have "maxed out," especially as the dispersion of minority voters from majority-minority districts made some other districts held by Republicans more competitive for the Democrats, and Democrats originally elected in majority-minority districts managed to get re-elected in new majority-majority districts. Whereas in earlier times, super-majority-minority districts were necessary to maximize minority election to legislative seats, recent findings indicate that sub-majority-minority districts are now optimal for minority representatives to be elected. Districts with 40–45 percent Black or minority voter presence will typically elect a minority representative while allowing more minority voters to be distributed to surrounding super-majority White districts, thus enhancing the chances of White Democrats to be elected (Epstein and O'Halloran, 1999, p. 190). If Republicans fail to win control of state legislatures in the South and the Department of Justice and the courts continue their move away from stringent majority-minority district requirements, Democrats may attempt to increase the number of districts with a potential to elect Democrats by reducing the proportion of minority voters in some current majority-minority districts to the 40–45 percent range.

On a national scale the implications of a leveling off or decline in the number of Republican House seats in the South does not augur well for continued Republican control of the House:

> Even in taking control of the House, Newt Gingrich's fellow southerners trailed the northern wing of the GOP. Only after several disaffected Democrats followed Georgian Nathan Deal's lead and shifted partisan allegiance did Republicans have a slightly larger share of the southern House seats (56 percent) than the non-southern (53 percent). In the 105th Congress, Republican House control rests entirely on the GOP's advantage in the South, where 59 percent of the seats are filled by Republicans; in the remainder of the nation, Democrats hold a one-seat majority. (Bullock and Rozell, 1998, pp. 7–8)

The non-presidential, off-year election in 1998 resulted in a net gain of five seats in the House for the president's party, something that had not occurred in over thirty years. Although the Republican party maintained its total of 71 U.S. House seats from Southern states, after the 1998 election they had 5 fewer House seats than the Democrats in the remainder of the country. The Republican majority in the House rested heavily on the majority of the Southern House seats because they held only 49 percent of the House seats outside the South after 1998.

It is also worth noting that in only three states—Florida, Alabama, and Tennessee—did the percentage vote for congressional candidates exceed the percentage of the vote for governor in the last election held. In only one state—Alabama—did the percentage of the vote for House candidates exceed that of the senatorial candidate in the last election. In other words, we can expect different voting outcomes as we move away from the presidential race and the electorate shrinks and changes as it moves down the ballot to more localized offices.

# Chapter 4

# Southern State Electoral Patterns

Southern governors have always been a colorful collection of individuals. On paper, most Southern governors are "weak" governors, holding few constitutional powers. In the South, power has traditionally resided with the state's legislature—a consequence of early and persistent distrust of executive authority dating from colonial times. As Southerners expanded westward, they tended to take this basic distrust of central authority and too much government with them. Part of the Southern political culture has been quite distinct from its Northern neighbors. The role of the political party in much of the North has been to integrate new arrivals (whether they be immigrants or young people coming of age) into the civic life of the community; however, in the South "virtually none of this was true of the factional system of old style Southern Democratic politics. Indeed, the emphasis was on keeping people out of politics, not on making them feel a part of the system" (Scher, 1997, p. 64). This exclusionary orientation not only extended to African Americans and other minorities, but to poor, non-landowning Whites as well. In a way, the lack of integration—both socially and politically—made the transformation of Southern politics easier if no less painful. It was not so much the allegiance to the Democratic political party that maintained the old system, but rather an allegiance to the oligarchic system of control. As legal, political, and social forces for change could no longer be resisted, the oligarchy simply found new ways to perpetuate itself. If this meant shifting political parties, then so be it.

Governors and state legislatures have been the key leaders for Southern states in responding to the forces of change in the latter half of the twentieth century, setting the approach to deal with change, and to create the milieu in which change occurred. It is at the state—this more localized level—that the differences among the Southern states emerge. It is also at this level that the national political balances and strategies will play out successfully or unsuccessfully.

## SOUTHERN GOVERNORS

Governors, somewhat like senators, hold statewide positions, but they lack the connection to national issues and policies that influence a Senate election. In most Southern states, gubernatorial elections have been moved from presidential election years, so that for the position of governor, the strength of the state GOP organization should be better reflected in the party's success at this purely state level. Only North Carolina holds gubernatorial elections in a presidential year. Three states—Mississippi, Virginia, and Louisiana—have taken the additional step of moving their gubernatorial elections to odd-numbered years to further insulate them from national electoral influences. The other eight states elect governors in the even-numbered, non-presidential years. Since 1986, all Southern states have moved to four-year terms for their governors.

Tables 4.1a and 4.1b, which present the results of elections for governor in the Peripheral South and Deep South since 1968, illustrate some interesting differences from the senatorial patterns. In recent years, no gubernatorial election has gone uncontested in the South with the exception of Louisiana (a unique system of elections allowing the bipartisan primary winner to assume office if she or he wins 50 percent of the vote in the primary).

The first victories achieved by Southern Republican gubernatorial candidates came in 1966 in Arkansas and Florida. Winthrop Rockefeller arrived in Arkansas in 1953 and began building and financing the Republican party. By 1966 he was able to capitalize on opposition within the Democratic party to former governor, Orval Faubus, and again in 1968 against a blatant Democratic racist candidate to win the governorship as a Republican. The reformist zeal of Rockefeller, his openly moderate position on most issues, including

**Table 4.1a**
**Number and Percent of Republican Wins in General Elections for Governor in the Peripheral South, 1968–1998**

| STATE/YEAR | '68 | '70 | '72 | '74 | '76 | '78 | '80 | '82 | '84 | '86 | '88 | '90 | '92 | '94 | '96 | '98 | TOTAL | % |
|---|---|---|---|---|---|---|---|---|---|---|---|---|---|---|---|---|---|---|
| Arkansas | R | D | D | D | D | D | R | D | D | D* | -- | D | -- | D | -- | R | 3 of 13 | 23.10% |
| Florida | -- | D | -- | D | -- | D | -- | D | -- | R | -- | D | -- | D | -- | R | 2 of 18 | 25.00% |
| North Carolina | D | -- | R | -- | D | -- | D | -- | R | -- | R | -- | D | -- | D | -- | 3 of 8 | 37.50% |
| Tennessee | -- | R | -- | D | -- | R | -- | R | -- | D | -- | D | -- | R | -- | R | 5 of 8 | 62.50% |
| Texas | D | D | D | D* | -- | R | -- | D | -- | R | -- | D | -- | R | -- | R | 4 of 10 | 36.40% |
| | | | | | | | | | | | | | | | | | | |
| Total Elections** | 3 | 5 | 3 | 5 | 2 | 5 | 2 | 5 | 2 | 5 | 1 | 5 | 1 | 5 | 1 | 5 | | |
| Total Won by Rep. | 1 | 2 | 1 | 1 | 0 | 3 | 1 | 1 | 1 | 2 | 1 | 0 | 0 | 3 | 0 | 5 | | |
| % Rep. Wins | 33% | 40% | 33% | 20% | 0% | 60% | 50% | 20% | 50% | 40% | 100% | 0% | 0% | 60% | 0% | 100% | | |
| | | | | | | | | | | | | | | | | | | |
| | | '69 | | '73 | | '77 | | '81 | | '85 | | '89 | | '93 | | '97 | | |
| Virginia | | R | | R | | R | | D | | D | | D | | R | | R | 5 of 8 | 62.50% |
| | | | | unop | | | | | | | | | | | | | | |

*Term increased 2–4 years; **Virginia's off-year election included in next year's total.

*Sources: Congressional Quarterly Reports;* Scammon, *America Votes*

**Table 4.1b**

**Number and Percent of Republican Wins in General Elections for Governor in the Deep South, 1967–1999**

| STATE/YEAR | '67 | '70 | '71 | '74 | '75 | '78 | '79 | '82 | '83 | '86 | '87 | '90 | '91 | '94 | '95 | '98 | '99 | TOTAL | % |
|---|---|---|---|---|---|---|---|---|---|---|---|---|---|---|---|---|---|---|
| Alabama | -- | D unop | -- | D | -- | D | -- | D | -- | R | -- | R | -- | R | -- | D | -- | 3 of 8 | 38% |
| Georgia | -- | D | -- | D | -- | D | -- | D | -- | D | -- | D | -- | D | -- | D | -- | 0 of 8 | 0% |
| South Carolina | -- | D | -- | R | -- | D | -- | D | -- | R | -- | R | -- | R | -- | D | -- | 4 of 8 | 50% |
| Total Elections | | 3 | | 3 | | 3 | | 3 | | 3 | | 3 | | 3 | | 3 | | | |
| Won by Rep. | | 0 | | 1 | | 0 | | 0 | | 2 | | 2 | | 2 | | 0 | | | |
| % of Rep. Wins | | 0% | | 33.3% | | 0% | | 0% | | 66.6% | | 66.6% | | 66.6% | | 0% | | | |
| Louisiana | D | -- | D | -- | D | -- | R | -- | D unop | -- | D unop | -- | D | -- | R | -- | R | 3 of 9 | 33% |
| Mississippi | D | -- | D unop | -- | D | -- | D | -- | D | -- | D | -- | R | -- | R | -- | D | 2 of 9 | 22% |
| Total Elections | 2 | | 2 | | 2 | | 2 | | 2 | | 2 | | 2 | | 2 | | 2 | | |
| Won by Rep. | 0 | | 0 | | 0 | | 1 | | 0 | | 0 | | 1 | | 2 | | 1 | | |
| % Rep. Wins | 0% | | 0% | | 0% | | 50% | | 0% | | 0% | | 50% | | 100% | | 50% | | |

*Sources: Scammon, America Votes; Congressional Quarterly Weekly Reports*

race, and the discontent of many Democrats over their own party's nominees, created Republican victories for the first time in Arkansas. Against a relatively unknown, moderate Democrat, Dale Bumpers, though, Rockefeller failed in his attempt to win a third term in 1970. With the Rockefeller administration beset with minor scandals, a moderate opponent and a united Democratic party returned the state to its historical pattern of electing Democratic governors. In 1972 the Republican share of the Arkansas gubernatorial vote fell to only 25 percent (see Figure 4.1).

The other gubernatorial victory in 1966 was in Florida, where Claude Kirk won by gaining conservative Democratic supporters opposed to the liberal, Democratic, big city mayor of Miami, Robert King High. It was a short-lived Republican victory. After a series of highly publicized antics, an abortive attempt to obtain the Republican vice presidential nomination, and a futile grandstand scene against the courts, Kirk was handily defeated by a united Democratic party under a banner of moderation. In addition, the popular, well-established GOP conservative Bill Cramer lost his bid for the Senate in 1970 against the rejuvenated Democratic party moderation that succeeded in uniting the "cracker" north and the Dade County (Miami) "liberals."

In 1969, Virginia added a third GOP governor to the Southern total, Linwood Holton. As in Rockefeller's victory, a combination of Blacks, regular Republicans, and liberal/moderate Democrats combined to elect a progressive Republican candidate for the first time in Virginia in the twentieth century. In 1973, conservative Democrat-turned Republican and former Holton foe, Mills Godwin, succeeded Holton by the narrowest of margins as a conservative alternative to the liberal Democrat-turned-Independent Henry Howell. With Howell actively discouraging a Democratic party endorsement, the Democratic party failed to even field a party candidate. Godwin, who had been elected previously as a Democrat, ran as a Republican with the support of Virginia's Independent political organization, the Byrd machine. Ideological differences heavily affected the outcome.

Although two of the sitting GOP governors in the South were defeated in 1970—Rockefeller and Kirk—Tennessee elected its first Republican governor since 1920, Winfield Dunn, running against a vulnerable Democratic candidate, John J. Hooker. North Carolina joined the list of Southern states by electing a Republican governor in 1972. James Holshouser, running as a progressive candidate,

# Figure 4.1
## Percentage of Republican Vote in General Elections for Governor, 1966–1999
(Note: zero percent = no Republican candidate)

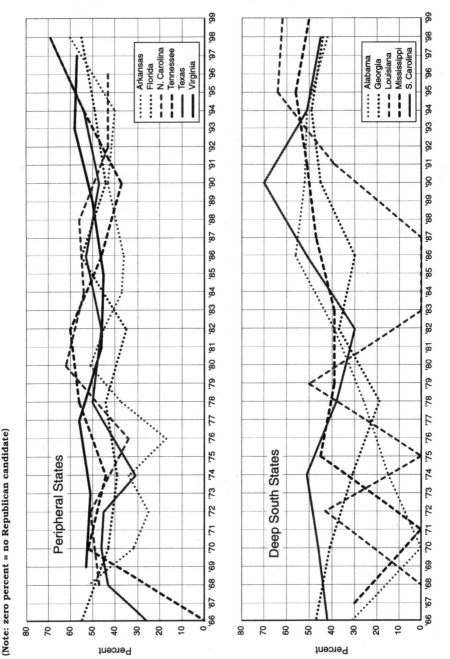

was elected by a narrow margin in the same state and year that an avowed arch-conservative, former-Democrat-turned-Republican Jesse Helms, won a Senate seat against a moderate to liberal Democrat. The "Nixon coattails" were credited with supplying the margin of victory for Holshouser, if not for both of the candidates. The 1972 election in North Carolina was a classic example of the bimodal electoral pattern in the Peripheral South states: very conservative, often former Democratic candidates (Helms), winning through activation of conservative, traditional White Democratic voters added to a Republican urban and mountain base and running against a perceived liberal (Galifianakis), versus traditional moderate Republicans (Holshouser) winning through activation of some Black and moderate to liberal Democrats alienated by very conservative Democratic nominees (Lake). Kazee calls this the traditionalist versus modernist conflict within North Carolina (Kazee, 1998, pp. 144–146).

In 1966 Georgia came very close to electing its and the Deep South's first Republican governor since Reconstruction. Howard "Bo" Calloway won a 3,000 vote plurality over Democrat Lester Maddox, but a write-in effort prevented any candidate from obtaining a majority. The state legislature, completely dominated by Democrats, elected Democrat Maddox. Calloway, a conservative, won many votes from moderate Democrats and urban voters strongly opposed to the avowed racist, Democratic candidate, but a liberal write-in campaign prevented Calloway from winning a majority (Murphy and Gulliver, 1971, pp. 4, 17). In Georgia, when gubernatorial candidates fail to win a majority of the vote in the general election, the state legislature elects the governor.

Prior to 1974, only candidates in the Peripheral South had been elected to the governor's office, despite Calloway's almost successful attempt in Georgia. In North Carolina, Virginia, Tennessee, and Florida moderate GOP candidates won by portraying their opponents as "liberals." In Georgia and Arkansas, moderately conservative Republican candidates garnered more votes than their Democratic opponents who had strong identification in the electorate as racists.

In 1974, South Carolina became the first Deep South state to elect a Republican governor, followed by Louisiana in 1979 and Alabama in 1986. After the 1994 election when Republicans gained control of the U.S. Congress, six of the eleven Southern states had Republican governors, three from Peripheral states—Tennessee,

Texas, and Virginia—and three from Deep South states—Alabama,
Mississippi, and South Carolina. Four years later, in 1998, there
were seven Republican governors in the South. Among Peripheral
South states, only North Carolina did not have a Republican gover-
nor, while in the Deep South, only Mississippi and Louisiana had
Republican governors.

The degree of electoral success among the states is quite different. Texas, which elected the first GOP senator in 1961, did not elect
a Republican governor until 1978, and then alternated between the
parties every four years from 1974 until 1994. In 1998, George W.
Bush became the first Texas governor to win re-election in twenty
years, and the first Republican governor to ever win two consecutive
terms in office.

Tennessee and Virginia have been the most consistent at the gubernatorial level for Republican victories. Tennessee voters appear
to switch parties every eight years, whereas Virginia voters have
switched between the parties every twelve years. North Carolina has
also alternated between the parties every eight years, but during most
of this time it has been heavily influenced by the presence of the
popular Democratic Governor James Hunt, who has occupied the
governor's office for sixteen years between 1976 and 1998. After
serving two terms from 1976 to 1984, he was prohibited by the state
constitution from serving another consecutive term. After an un-
successful try for the U.S. Senate in 1984, he was re-elected governor in 1992 and again in 1996.

Among Peripheral South states, only Arkansas and Florida have
maintained the pattern of Democratic governors with occasional
Republican inroads. Arkansas has had only two Republican governors since 1968, but now has a third Republican governor due to
the resignation of the incumbent Democratic governor because of
legal problems. Florida has had only one Republican governor since
1968; however in 1998, the incumbent Democratic governor had to
retire and Jeb Bush, the former president's son and Republican gubernatorial candidate in 1994, won the seat. Having run a very
strong race against the incumbent in 1994, benefiting from a split
within the Democratic party and the lack of a strong, dynamic
Democratic candidate worked to elect Republican Bush on his second attempt for the governorship.

Among the Deep South states, only South Carolina has had a
consistent pattern of Republican success for the governor's position, having elected Republicans in gubernatorial elections half the

time since 1968. However, in 1998 a string of three consecutive Republican victories ended with the defeat of incumbent David Beasley by Democrat Jim Hodges, who championed a controversial but popular proposal for a state lottery. Alabama has elected three Republican governors, and Mississippi two Republicans governors since 1967, including two of the three most recent races in Mississippi. In Alabama's 1994 election, a former Democratic governor who switched to the Republican party narrowly defeated the incumbent Democratic governor who had not been elected to office, but who had succeeded the former Republican governor when he resigned on conviction of campaign finance abuse. In the 1998 race, the incumbent Republican Governor Fob James was defeated by Don Siegelman who, like Democrat Hodges in South Carolina, campaigned in favor of a popular proposal for a state lottery. In both South Carolina and Alabama, the incumbent Republicans counted heavily on the support of conservative Christian voters for their re-elections, but both failed in their attempts to remain in office.

In 1999, Mississippi had a very close gubernatorial election that ended the Republican trend in the governor's office the previous two elections. With incumbent Republican Kirk Fordice unable to run for re-election, Democratic Lieutenant Governor Ronnie Musgrove received more votes than his Republican challenger, but failed to win fifty percent of the vote.

Louisiana has only elected two Republicans since the 1960s, including the current incumbent. In the Louisiana all-party primary runoff in 1995, it took former Congressman Mike Foster running against an African American Democrat, who failed to receive strong support from his own party, to become the state's first Republican governor since 1979 and only the second in this century. Foster was re-elected easily in 1999 by winning 62 percent of the vote in the all-party primary.

Georgia is the only Southern state that has not elected a Republican governor. In 1994, however, the narrowest of margins kept incumbent Democrat Zell Miller in office against the strong challenge of Republican businessman Guy Millner. Miller's championing of the Hope Scholarships for Georgia high school students to attend college is credited with providing the edge in his re-election. Miller had to retire in 1998 under the state's constitutional limit on terms. Republican Millner made a second attempt to win the governor's office in 1998 against Democrat Roy Barnes, who enjoyed the support of retiring Governor Zell Miller and former President Jimmy Carter.

Barnes won a surprising 56 percent of the vote in what many had expected to be a Republican victory for a Democratic governor's seat.

A Democratic resurgence at the gubernatorial level appeared to occur in the Deep South with the 1998 election: two incumbent Republican governors were defeated and a governor's office was retained in a state (Georgia) that was expected to vote Republican. Running against a Republican trend, Georgia Democrats retained the governor's office in 1998, while Republicans re-elected incumbent Senator Paul Coverdell and eight of the eleven Republican congressioal candidates. The Republican trend in Georgia was also evident at presidential level with the switch in support from Democrat Clinton in 1992 to support for Republican Dole in 1996. The Peripheral South, on the other hand, demonstrated a Republican sweep of governors' offices up for election in 1998. No winning candidate for governor in the South in 1998 won with less than 55 percent of the vote, which is typically used to define a "safe" seat.

Because gubernatorial races are statewide races, the issues of district makeup are not as important to electoral success as they are in the House or state legislative races. Unlike the Senate races, however, electoral contests for governor are influenced heavily by more localized state interests. Social conservatism is prevalent across the South, and although there is variation among the states—gaming may be acceptable in Mississippi or Virginia and not in North Carolina—successful candidates espouse conservative positions on most social issues.

A second characteristic that increasingly emerges in Southern gubernatorial races is the role of the governor as economic booster for the state. This translates into a prerequisite of fiscal conservatism, but with an ability to leverage the state's resources to achieve greater economic growth and prosperity within the state. In the South this is not an assumption of the state going into business, but rather, an illustration of the state's governor working to allow business to flourish with few constraints, thus attracting new businesses and encouraging existing businesses to expand. In many instances this also translates into permissible state spending for highways, bridges, and infrastructure, as well as for education and job training to better prepare the state's workforce.

Finally, gubernatorial elections often become the ground for intra-party conflicts between the country club/modernist/bourbon/moderate members of the party and the traditionalist/Christian Right/extreme conservative members of the party who fundamentally focus on religion. The competition between these two groups is prevalent in the Republican party. Among Democrats the extreme conservative group has devolved to a point where it typically is not a major factor in candidate selection any more.

Increasingly, the Religious Right has become the dominant player in the selection of Republican candidates. In Virginia, the Religious Right controls the state party organization and the party's convention. In 1996 the Virginia Republican party convention voted by a three-to-one margin to nominate a Christian Right candidate rather than incumbent John Warner for the U.S. Senate seat. Because incumbent Senator John Warner expected to lose the nominating vote at the party's state convention, he called for a party primary election under an obscure portion of state law to avoid certain defeat at the Republican party's state convention. Incumbent Warner won the party's nomination in the primary by a two-to-one margin and was then re-elected easily in the general election (Rozell, 1998, pp. 134–135).

In Louisiana in 1995, Christian Right voters rallied around Mike Foster in the primary, denying the well-known Democrat-turned-Republican Buddy Roemer a position on the run-off ballot, and then sweeping to a strong victory over the seriously split Democrats and their African American gubernatorial candidate. In South Carolina, Democrat-turned-Republican David Beasley captured his new party's nomination and then won a narrow victory over Democratic Lieutenant Governor Nick Theodore, by strongly wooing the Christian Right.

For Republican Southern gubernatorial candidates, social conservatism, economic/business entrepreneurism, and religious fundamentalism appear increasingly to be prerequisites for successfully winning the party's nomination. The religious fundamentalism portion of the formula will be the touchstone for the Republican party in the next decades and the point of potential division and defeat for Republican candidates when it bursts to the forefront of campaigns. As Figure 4.2 presents, many Republican governors have been elected with marginal percentages, often based on splits in the Democratic party or the unique personality characteristics of either the Republican or Democratic candidate. A particularly divisive primary split within the Republican ranks over religious issues, which creates a perception among voters that the Republican nominee is too extreme, will likely spell defeat. The religious split is somewhat obviated by the fact that the Democratic nominees for governor in some instances have been more moderate, or less conservative on social and religious issues than even the non–Christian Right Republican candidates, or at least have been successfully portrayed as such because of particular groups that support the Democratic nominee. Therefore, conservative Christians often have nowhere else to go other than to support the Republican candidate even if that person is not their first choice, or to stay home and abstain from voting, which risks the election of a candidate even less to their liking than the non–Christian Right Republican candidate. The need to win conservative Christian voters in Republican primaries draws Republican candidates to more conservative positions on social and religious issues; whereas the need to garner minority voters for Democratic candidates to win their party's nomination attracts Democratic candidates with more liberal positions than many middle-of-the-road Southern voters are willing to support.

In relation to comparable senatorial races, the earliest successful GOP governors tended to be equally, or more, moderate than their Democratic rivals, whereas successful senatorial candidates have more often than not been the more conservative candidates. Since the 1970s, however, Southern voters have tended to support gubernatorial candidates who portray an image of fiscal conservatism and social moderation, except on crime, regardless of party affiliation. In the 1990s, being too liberal or too conservative tended to hamper chances of election to a governorship in the South. Although moderation is preferable to liberalism (for example, the 1996 Texas gubernatorial race when Republican George W. Bush defeated incumbent Democrat Ann Richards by 8 percent), when presented with a choice between conservatism and liberalism, conservatism will usually win (for example, the 1993 Virginia governor's race when Republican George Allen defeated Democrat Mary Sue Terry by almost 18 percentage points).

Differences do persist among the Peripheral and Deep South states, but there is also convergence. Since 1990, Republicans have won eight of the seventeen governors' races in the Peripheral South, including all of the last five; Republicans in the Deep South states have won eight of the fifteen gubernatorial races in that same time period, but lost four of the last five races.

In 1998, seven Southern governors' seats were up for reelection—five held by Republicans and two by Democrats. Both incumbent Democrats were barred from seeking re-election. All five

Republican seats had incumbents running for re-election. Given the disarray among the Democrats in Arkansas and the weak position of the Democratic parties in Georgia and Florida during the 1994 gubernatorial elections, Republicans were expected to win all seven seats, which would have raised their total of Southern governorships to ten of the eleven possible positions. The eleventh governor's position is in North Carolina, the lone Southern state that elects its governor in presidential election years. As it turned out, Republicans won only one of the open seats—Florida—and lost two of their incumbents—Alabama and South Carolina.

In 1999, the two Southern states that have gubernatorial elections in odd-numbered years–Mississippi and Louisiana–were both held by Republicans. In Louisiana's all-party primary, incumbent Republican Mike Foster easily defeated several challengers with 62 percent of the vote. In Mississippi, where term limits prohibited Republican Kirk Fordice from running a third time, a very close election resulted. The Republican party's prospects were not helped prior to the election by the out-going governor's admission of an affair with a woman while he was governor, and his wife's intent to divorce him. Democratic Lieutenant Governor Ronnie Musgrove faced former Republican Congressman Mike Parker and two minor party candidates. Although Musgrove received more votes than Parker, he did not receive a majority of the votes cast because of the minor party candidates. Mississippi's constitution requires that the governor must win a majority of the votes cast as well as majority of the 122 Mississippi state legislative house districts. If no candidate wins the majorities required, the state house of representatives elects the governor. In the same 1999 election, 86 Democrats and 33 Republicans were elected to the Mississippi house. In January 2000, the solidly Democratic house elected Democrat Musgrove governor.

Republicans can be competitive in every Southern state at the state level in gubernatorial elections, although the successful candidate, whether Democrat or Republican, relies much more heavily upon candidate personality, image, and "local" issues than on national trends and concerns.

## STATE LEGISLATURES

More than any other elective office, the state legislative contests signal the bedrock position of political parties within a state. More than the governor, state legislatures are still where the power resides within states across the South. In order for the Republican party in a state in the South to be truly competitive, it must elect members to state legislatures.

State legislative races are subject to some of the same influences as U.S. House contests in that they are subject to reapportionment after every census and must conform to one person, one vote guidelines. In addition, in the nine Southern states subject to review of their legislative districting, the trend in the U.S. Department of Justice to insist on the creation of majority-minority districts, and the trend in the federal courts to retreat from majority-minority districts has affected the composition of state legislatures. State legislative seats, though, are also very local. State legislative districts are typically small and homogeneous. The state legislator is usually known to many people in the district because the person lives and works in the district, has done so for years prior to seeking office, and shares similar activities and concerns with others in the district. Because state legislative positions are considered part-time positions and state legislative sessions tend to be relatively short, especially among Southern states, the legislator spends much more time in the specific area he or she represents than do congressional representatives or governors. Friends and neighbors and local issues along with state issues are more salient for voters in electing state legislative candidates. Unlike local mayoral, council, and county commission races that are frequently non-partisan, state legislative races provide a local-level partisan picture that can be aggregated statewide.

Although state legislative races are an indicator of political party strength at a grassroots level within a state, it is the case that most state legislative races occur in even-numbered years and thus are to a degree subject to broader national trends and variations in turnout and interest related to the more highly visible and publicized national or statewide candidates and races. Typically, in a presidential election year, the president's party gains 117 state legislative seats on average nationally. Since the 1960s, the three exceptions have been Nixon in 1972 (a loss of 7 state legislative seats overall), Carter in 1976 (a loss of 22 seats), and Clinton in 1992 (a loss of 150 seats). In 1996 Democrats had a gain of 53 state legislative seats over 1994. "The Johnson and Reagan landslides of 1964 and 1984 generated major state legislative gains for their parties, but the large margins won by Nixon in 1972 and Bush in 1988 did not" (National Conference of State Legislatures, "Democratic Share," 1996, p. 1).

In midterm election years when there is no presidential race occurring nationally, the party of the president has experienced a net loss of state legislative seats in every non-presidential election year since 1962. Presidential election years draw voters to the polls who don't normally vote in other types of elections, for example, state legislative elections when there is no presidential election. On average, regardless of the party in the White House, nationally 307 state legislative seats are lost in midterm election years by the president's party. In 1998, for the first time in thirty-six years, the party of the president gained seats in the off-year election. Republicans experienced a net loss of 37 state legislative seats nationally, losing four legislative chambers—the Wisconsin senate, North Carolina house, New Hampshire senate and the Washington senate, and the tied Indiana house to Democratic control. Republicans gained control of two chambers from the Democrats—the Michigan house and the Minnesota house.

In 1998, the Republican party experienced a net loss of 37 state legislative seats nationally. Since 1968, Republicans have gained seats in state legislatures as they have at other levels of government in the South (see Tables 4.2a and 4.2b). Tennessee and Florida have exhibited the earliest and most sustained Republican presence. The virtual absence of Southern Republican state legislators is apparent in the 1970s and 1980s. Although gradual increases in the number of Republican legislators occur in most Southern states, it is only in the 1990s that Republican success becomes clearly noticeable.

By 1988, Florida and Tennessee Republicans were electing approximately 40 percent of state legislators, whereas Virginia, North Carolina, and Texas were electing a third in one or more legislative chambers (see Figures 4.2a and 4.2b). By 1992, Florida Republicans had achieved a tie in their state senate; South Carolina, Tennessee, Texas, and Virginia were breaking 40 percent; North Carolina had stalled around 30 percent; and Georgia, Alabama, and Mississippi had moved into the 20 percent range. The 1994 election was a breakthrough election for Republicans in some state legislatures, as it was in congressional elections in the South, with a majority of the seats in the Florida senate and the North Carolina house being won by Republican legislative candidates, and a tie with the Democrats occurring in the South Carolina house. Most other Southern states witnessed modest, if any, Republican gains. Given the sweeping changes at the congressional level, it is surprising that more change did not occur at the state legislative level.

## Table 4.2a
## Number of Republican and Total State Legislative House of Representatives Seats in South, 1970–1999

| STATE | 1970 | 1972 | 1974 | 1976 | 1978 | 1980 | 1982 | 1984 | 1986 | 1988 | 1990 | 1992 | 1994 | 1996 | 1998 |
|---|---|---|---|---|---|---|---|---|---|---|---|---|---|---|---|
| **Total Seats** | | | | | | | | | | | | | | | |
| Alabama 105 | 2 | 2 | 0 | 2 | 4 | 4 | 8 | 12 | 16 | 17 | 23 | 23 | 31 | 34 | 36 |
| Arkansas 100 | 2 | 1 | 2 | 5 | 6 | 7 | 7 | 9 | 9 | 11 | 9 | 10 | 12 | 13 | 23 |
| Florida 120 | 38 | 42 | 34 | 27 | 31 | 39 | 36 | 43 | 45 | 47 | 46 | 49 | 57 | 61 | 72 |
| Georgia 180 | 22 | 29 | 24 | 24 | 21 | 23 | 14 | 26 | 27 | 36 | 35 | 52 | 65 | 74 | 78 |
| Louisiana 105 | 1 | 4 | 4 | 4 | 9 | 10 | 11 | 14 | 15 | 17 | 16 | 16 | 17 | 28 | 27 |
| Mississippi 122 | 2 | 2 | 2 | 3 | 4 | 4 | 5 | 6 | 9 | 9 | 23 | 27 | 31 | 33 | 36/33* |
| N. Carolina 120 | 23 | 35 | 9 | 6 | 15 | 24 | 18 | 38 | 36 | 46 | 39 | 42 | 68 | 61 | 54 |
| S. Carolina 124 | 11 | 21 | 17 | 12 | 16 | 17 | 20 | 27 | 32 | 37 | 42 | 50 | 62 | 70 | 68 |
| Tennessee 99 | 43 | 48 | 35 | 32 | 38 | 39 | 37 | 37 | 38 | 40 | 42 | 36 | 40 | 38 | 40 |
| Texas 150 | 10 | 17 | 16 | 9 | 22 | 35 | 36 | 52 | 56 | 57 | 57 | 58 | 61 | 68 | 71 |
| Virginia 100 | 23 | 20 | 17 | 21 | 25 | 35 | 34 | 33 | 35 | 39 | 41 | 41 | 47 | 47 | 49/52* |

*Seats in 1998/Seats after 1999 election

Source: National Conference of State Legislatures

82

**Table 4.2b**

**Number of Republican and Total State Legislative Senate Seats in South, 1970–1999**

| STATE | 1970 | 1972 | 1974 | 1976 | 1978 | 1980 | 1982 | 1984 | 1986 | 1988 | 1990 | 1992 | 1994 | 1996 | 1998 |
|---|---|---|---|---|---|---|---|---|---|---|---|---|---|---|---|
| Total Seats | | | | | | | | | | | | | | | |
| Alabama 35 | 0 | 0 | 0 | 0 | 0 | 0 | 3 | 4 | 5 | 6 | 7 | 7 | 12 | 12 | 12 |
| Arkansas 35 | 1 | 1 | 1 | 1 | 0 | 1 | 3 | 4 | 4 | 4 | 4 | 5 | 7 | 6 | 6 |
| Florida 40 | 13 | 14 | 12 | 9 | 11 | 13 | 8 | 8 | 15 | 17 | 18 | 20 | 21 | 23 | 25 |
| Georgia 56 | 6 | 8 | 5 | 4 | 5 | 5 | 7 | 9 | 10 | 11 | 11 | 15 | 20 | 22 | 23 |
| Louisiana 39 | 1 | 1 | 1 | 1 | 0 | 0 | 1 | 1 | 5 | 5 | 5 | 4 | 6 | 14 | 14 |
| Mississippi 52 | 2 | 2 | 2 | 2 | 4 | 4 | 3 | 3 | 7 | 8 | 9 | 13 | 14 | 18 | 18/18* |
| N. Carolina 50 | 7 | 15 | 1 | 3 | 5 | 10 | 6 | 12 | 10 | 13 | 14 | 11 | 24 | 20 | 15 |
| S. Carolina 46 | 2 | 3 | 2 | 3 | 2 | 5 | 6 | 10 | 10 | 11 | 12 | 16 | 17 | 20 | 20 |
| Tennessee 33 | 13 | 13 | 12 | 9 | 12 | 12 | 11 | 10 | 10 | 11 | 13 | 14 | 15 | 15 | 15 |
| Texas 31 | 2 | 3 | 3 | 4 | 4 | 7 | 11 | 10 | 6 | 8 | 9 | 13 | 14 | 15 | 16 |
| Virginia 40 | 7 | 6 | 5 | 5 | 9 | 9 | 8 | 8 | 10 | 10 | 18 | 18 | 18 | 20 | 21/21* |

*Seats in 1998/Seats after 1999 election

*Source:* National Conference of State Legislatures

83

**Figure 4.2a**
**Percentage of State House Seats Held by Republicans in the South, 1966–1999**

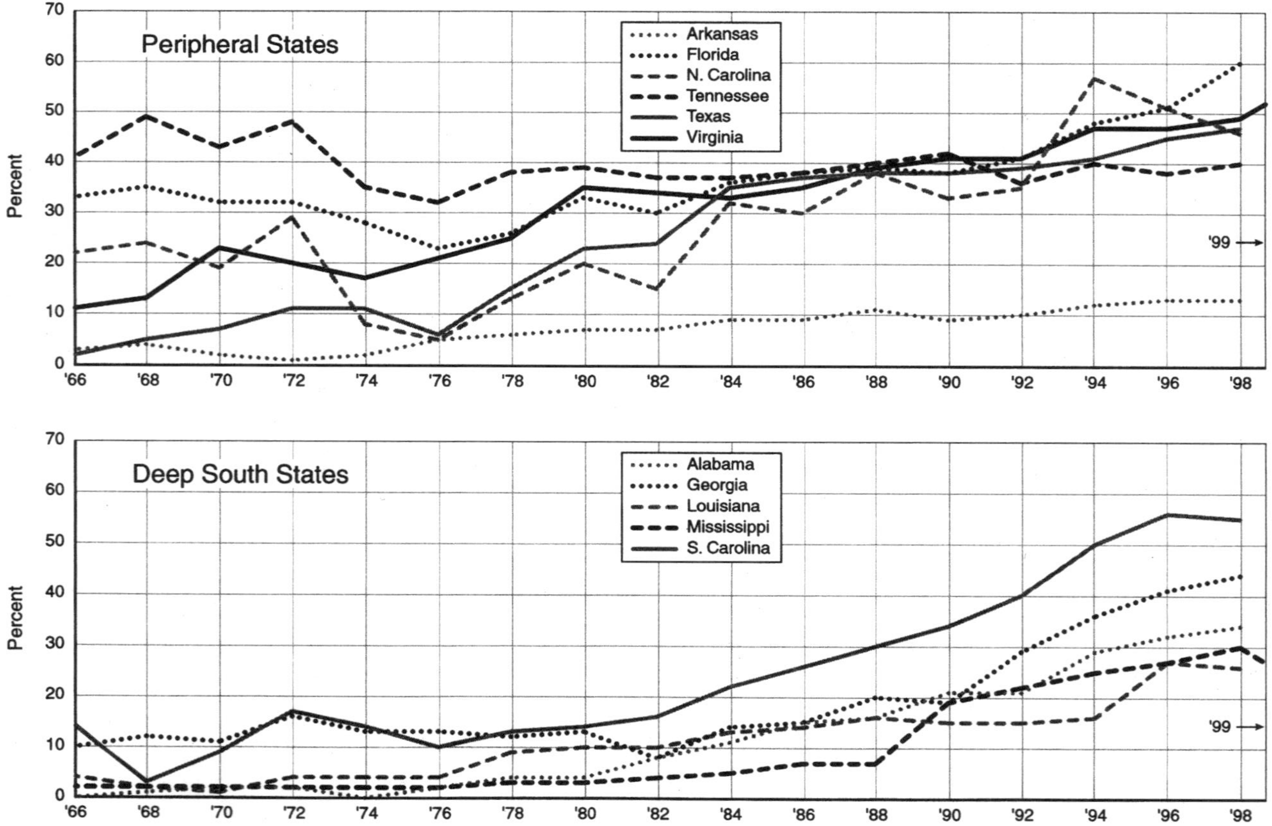
Peripheral States
Arkansas
Florida
N. Carolina
Tennessee
Texas
Virginia
Percent
70
60
50
40
30
20
10
0
'66
'68
'70
'72
'74
'76
'78
'80
'82
'84
'86
'88
'90
'92
'94
'96
'98
'99 →
Deep South States
Alabama
Georgia
Louisiana
Mississippi
S. Carolina

Figure 4.2b
Percentage of State Senate Seats Held by Republicans in the South, 1966–1999

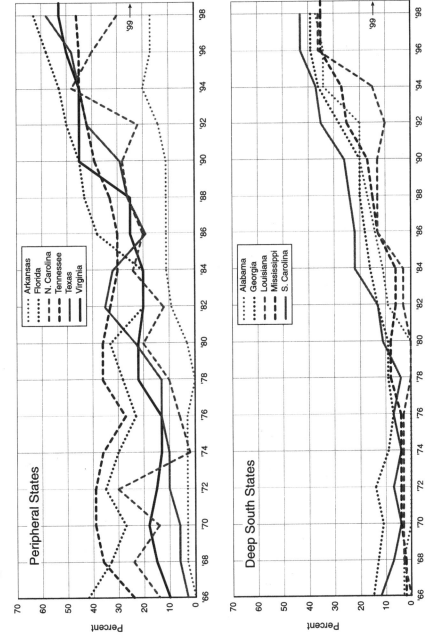

In 1996, Republicans either held their own or increased the proportion of seats held in every Southern state except Arkansas and North Carolina where Republicans lost seats in the Arkansas senate and both houses in North Carolina. After the 1998 election, Republicans continued to increase their state legislative seats across the South with the exception again of both houses in North Carolina and the Louisiana and South Carolina state houses. In North Carolina, the Republicans lost control of the state house, which they had captured in the 1994 election. In Florida in 1998 and Virginia in 1999, for the first time in the South since Reconstruction, Republicans controlled both houses of the state legislature and the governorship at the same time. Democrats continued to control both legislative chambers in Alabama, Arkansas, Georgia, Louisiana, Mississippi, North Carolina, and Tennessee. Republicans held the South Carolina house and the Texas and Virginia senates. In 1999, Republicans lost seats in the Mississippi house.

Nationally, the Democratic party has enjoyed control of a majority of the legislative chambers in the 49 partisan states for the past 36 years (see Table 4.3). Nebraska is the only state that has a nonpartisan legislature. In 1994, for the first time, Republicans gained control of more state legislatures than the Democrats, winning control in 19 states. Democrats controlled 18 states, and 12 were split. After the 1994 election, Republicans controlled 50 of the 98 partisan state senate and house legislative chambers, the Democrats held 46, and 2 were tied.

In 1996, the Democrats regained their edge, gaining or maintaining control of both legislative houses in 20 states and leaving the Republicans in control of 18 states with 11 split. With a net shift of only 53 seats out of over 7,400 state legislative seats nationally as a result of the 1996 election, Democrats controlled 50 state legislative chambers, Republicans dropped to 46, and 2 were tied (National Conference of State Legislatures, "Partisan Control," 1996, p. 1).

After the 1998 non-presidential election, Republicans held control of only 45 legislative chambers nationwide, Democrats controlled 52 chambers, 1 was tied (Washington house), and 1 was a unicameral, non-partisan legislature—Nebraska (National Conference of State Legislatures, "1998 Election," 1998). In 1999, Republicans gained control of one more chamber—the Virginia House of Delegates.

Prior to the 1994 election, Republicans controlled 29 percent of the state legislative seats in the South compared to 47 percent in

**Table 4.3**
**Partisan Control of All State Legislative Chambers, 1966–1999**

| Election Year | Number of States | | |
|---|---|---|---|
| | Democrat | Republican | Split |
| 1966 | 23 | 16 | 9 |
| 1968 | 20 | 20 | 8 |
| 1970 | 23 | 16 | 9 |
| 1972 | 26 | 16 | 7 |
| 1974 | 37 | 4 | 8 |
| 1976 | 35 | 4 | 10 |
| 1978 | 31 | 11 | 7 |
| 1980 | 29 | 15 | 5 |
| 1982 | 34 | 11 | 4 |
| 1984 | 26 | 11 | 12 |
| 1986 | 28 | 9 | 12 |
| 1988 | 29 | 8 | 12 |
| 1990 | 30 | 6 | 13 |
| 1992 | 25 | 8 | 16 |
| 1994 | 18 | 19 | 12 |
| 1996 | 20 | 18 | 11 |
| 1998 | 21 | 17 | 11 |
| 1999 | 19 | 18 | 12 |

*Source*: National Conference of State Legislatures

non-Southern states. After the 1994 election, Republicans still controlled only 34 percent of the Southern legislative seats, but 54 percent of the seats in non-Southern states. The increase in Republican fortunes was a similar 7 percent both inside and outside the South (National Conference of State Legislatures, "Democratic Share," 1996, p. 1). In 1996, 1998, and 1999 Republican strength in the South continued to rise, while in the non-South, Republican state legislative strength has declined (see Table 4.4). After the 1999 election, Republicans held only 49 percent of the state legislative seats outside the South, but had increased their proportion of legislative seats in the South to 42 percent. Republicans have experienced a drop of 5 percent in the number of seats held outside the South since their successful 1994 election year, but have witnessed a 6 percent increase in seats held in the South, continuing a recent trend of reliance upon a Southern regional electoral base.

**Table 4.4**
**Republican Percentage of All State Legislative Seats Nationally,**
**1966–1999**

| Election Year | All States | Southern States | Non-Southern States |
|---|---|---|---|
| 1966 | 41 | 16 | 54 |
| 1968 | 43 | 17 | 62 |
| 1970 | 39 | 16 | 51 |
| 1972 | 40 | 19 | 50 |
| 1974 | 32 | 14 | 41 |
| 1976 | 32 | 13 | 42 |
| 1978 | 36 | 16 | 46 |
| 1980 | 40 | 18 | 50 |
| 1982 | 32 | 17 | 47 |
| 1984 | 42 | 22 | 51 |
| 1986 | 40 | 23 | 48 |
| 1988 | 40 | 25 | 47 |
| 1990 | 39 | 26 | 46 |
| 1992 | 41 | 29 | 47 |
| 1994 | 48 | 36 | 54 |
| 1996 | 47 | 38 | 51 |
| 1998 | 47 | 39 | 51 |
| 1999 | 47 | 42 | 49 |

*Source*: National Conference of State Legislatures

In the eight Southern states that had legislative elections in 1994, Arkansas, Georgia, the South Carolina house, Tennessee, and the Texas house returned over 90 percent of their incumbents running for re-election. In Alabama's senate, in Florida, and in the Texas senate, 87–89 percent of incumbents were re-elected. Only in the Alabama house and the North Carolina senate did the percentage of incumbents drop to 80–81 percent, and to 74 percent in the North Carolina house (National Conference of State Legislatures, "Partisan Control," 1996). Nationally, over 90 percent of incumbents were re-elected to their state legislative seats.

Did most of the "Republican Revolution" class of 1994 retain their seats in 1996? Yes. Nationally, there was a 20 percent turnover in state legislative seats between 1994 and 1996. In the South, six states had lower turnover rates; Arkansas equaled the national average; and three states exceeded 20 percent—Louisiana = 31 percent, South Carolina = 22 percent, and North Carolina = 21 percent. In Louisiana, the higher turnover rate added to the Republican party growth, although it built on a very low base. In South Carolina, the turnover strengthened the Republican control of the house and its minority in the senate. North Carolina moved in the opposite direction by whittling away at the Republican majority in the house and increasing the majority Democratic control in the senate (National Conference of State Legislatures, "Partisan Control," 1996).

At this most basic partisan level, this frequent springboard for higher statewide and national office, the Democratic party continues to dominate Southern state legislatures, but for the first time in this century, Republicans control both houses of the Florida and Virginia state legislatures, the state house of representatives in South Carolina, and the state senate in Texas. Republicans are poised to take over both houses of the legislature in Texas, and possibly one chamber in Georgia and Tennessee. In Arkansas, Republican prospects are bleak. In the remaining states—Alabama, Mississippi, Louisiana, and North Carolina—Democrats appear to be holding their own, with the Republicans losing control of the house in North Carolina and falling below a third of the seats in the state senate.

All indications, though, suggest that the top-down trickle of Republican voting behavior has reached the state legislative level and is growing. At the state legislative level, the rate of change has been slower and the results less sweeping. "Republicans are clearly becoming more like their Democratic counterparts in the areas of contestation and competition, if not always in seat gains, though it is clear that the capacity to contest and become competitive is a critical element for *future* success" (Anderson, 1997, p. 180).

If the fortunes of the Democrats nationally continue to reverse earlier Republican trends, then Democrats may indeed continue their control of state legislative bodies in the South as voters find support for Democrats more beneficial than in the past. The fact that Democrats continue to dominate most Southern legislative districts suggests that the conversion to the Republican party has not been absolute or complete. If Republicans fail to maintain and consolidate their majority position in Congress or to regain the presidency in the year 2000, their success in the state legislatures may also stall and falter. But even at this level, two-party competition has emerged, especially in Peripheral South states. In Chapter 5 we will examine indices of party competition at various electoral levels in the South.

*Chapter 5*

# Indices of Party Competition

What conclusions can we draw from the preceding discussions of the relative competitiveness of the Republican party in the South? Which one of these indicators is the "best" one to use in trying to examine party competition? Which is a true reflection of the status of the two parties in a particular state? Over the years, several researchers have made attempts to determine which indicator is the most reliable, which method is the most useful for treating the data, and what data are most valid as a focus of study in this area.

## EARLY ATTEMPTS TO MEASURE PARTY COMPETITION

In his studies of partisan competition in the fifty states, Ranney was most interested in determining the degree of competitiveness for state offices. He combined (1) the average percentage of the vote cast for Democratic gubernatorial candidates, (2) the average percentage of seats held by Democrats in the state senate, (3) the average percentage of seats held by Democrats in the state house of representatives, and (4) the percentage of all possible terms for governor, state senate, and state house won by the Democrats. On the basis of the scores obtained as a result of these computations for the years 1956–1970, Ranney determined that Louisiana (.9877), Alabama (.9685), Mississippi (.9407), South Carolina (.9292), Texas (.9132), Georgia (.9080), and Arkansas (.8850) were one-party Democratic states, and North Carolina (.8332), Virginia (.8235), Florida (.8052), and Tennessee (.7942) were modified one-party Democratic states (Ranney, 1971, p. 87).

Ranney and Kendall (1954) used a similar procedure to illustrate that competition varied among the fifty states. There are, however, some difficulties in using their method of computation. By combining percentage of elections and percentage of votes, a certain amount of imprecision and non-comparability are introduced. David Pfeiffer maintained that this problem could be overcome by dropping the percentage of elections won and simply concentrating on the percentage vote. In this manner the computation was simplified, as was the presentation of results. By using percentage of the vote, the results were open to a broad range of parametric statistics and tests that could not be applied to the Ranney figures (Pfeiffer, 1967, p. 462). In addition, Pfeiffer rejected the use of the "pendulum" effect, or the number of times the two parties took turns winning a particular office. He found that this measure too was an imprecise measure, not suitable for complex analysis (1967, p. 460). Instead, Pfeiffer used the average percentage of the vote won in elections for president, U.S. senator, governor, and one other statewide office. For the years 1940 to 1964, Pfeiffer was interested in measuring the trends away from, or toward, two-party competition and the persistence of party competition within a state—two of the major concerns of this study.

Pfeiffer's procedure appears to have problems as well. The use of the presidential vote distorts the strength/weakness of the party in a state, particularly in the South where by all accounts party competition at any level other than the presidential level has been mostly non-existent over long periods of time. In addition, presidential voting has been much more subject to third-party distortions than state and local races, at least in the South. There is also a problem with the "other statewide offices" category since Republicans rarely offered candidates for these offices, and seldom had they been elected. The usefulness of low "n" categories—categories where there are very few election contests to examine—is questionable.

Performance of a party at the statewide level below the governor's office is indeed a useful indicator of the vitality of a party organization because it demonstrates the voters' willingness to give partisan control over local and state policies and laws. Evidence of electoral success for offices that can be easily compared among the Southern states is needed to discuss party competition throughout the region. Pfeiffer acknowledged this problem and modified his earlier index by substituting aggregated U.S. House voting returns for the other statewide office category (1967, p. 462).

Paul T. David developed three similar indices to measure party competition: Composite A, which included the percentage vote for president, governor, U.S. Senate, and U.S. House of Representatives; Composite B, which included the percentage vote for governor, U.S. Senate, and U.S. House; and Composite C, which only included the percentage vote for U.S. Senate and U.S. House (*Party*, 1972, Chap. 3). Of these three composites, David concluded that Composite B was the best index of party strength at the state level because it included a range of votes that could be aggregated for statewide offices and that avoided the distortion of national and international issues associated with presidential elections (*Party*, 1972, pp. 16–17).

David emphasized the importance of biennial time series data in order to create sufficient data points to compare trends and results over time, a need that Pfeiffer (1967) and Cox (1960) also recognized in their earlier studies. Examining trends in party competition based on every four years, especially presidential years, missed more subtle and gradual shifts in statewide electoral patterns.

The problem of varying terms of office for different states and different offices was overcome by using the total number of votes cast for one candidate for an office in a given year, divided by the total number of votes cast for all candidates for that office. For years when no election was held for a particular office, a percentage was obtained by averaging the percentage of the vote for that office in the preceding election year and the election that immediately followed. In this manner a biennial time series was created for each state that provided a reliable picture for two offices elected on a statewide basis (governor and U.S. senator), plus a third (U.S. representative) that could be easily aggregated on a statewide basis. Presidential voting "tends to depart most widely from other voting in the states with the highest scores for variance of all kinds. These are predominantly the one-party states of the South" (David, *Party*, 1972, p. 23). For this reason, presidential voting was presented separately by David.

In order to understand the patterns of competition within the Southern states and differences in competitive patterns at different electoral levels, the election results in the Southern states are exam-

ined. The relatively simple and straightforward indices of party competition provide a useful picture of the trends across the South in
the ebb and flow of political party support among voters. The bottom
line is that political parties and their candidates judge their success
by getting enough votes to win elections. It is only when candidates
win elections and their numbers among elected officials increase
that much attention is paid to the position and prospects of political
parties. There is no doubt that Republican candidates can now win
elections in the South. The question remains, though, to what extent are the two main parties competitive over time and how far
down the ticket does competition extend within Southern states?

## PARTY COMPETITION IN THE SOUTH

Competition Index scores were calculated to demonstrate patterns and trends within the states. By taking the total number of Republican votes cast for specified offices and dividing by the total
number of votes cast for all candidates for that office and then multiplying by 2, an index score ranging from 0.0 to 2.0 results that can
be used to discuss the competitive position of the two major parties.

Figure 5.1 presents Competition Index scores for presidential
elections for the period 1968–1996. Scores range from 0.0 (perfect
Democratic dominance) to 2.0 (perfect Republican dominance).
Categories of competition can also be developed from the Competition scores that reflect degrees of partisan competition. Using a
standard definition of "competitive" seats as any election in which
the winning candidate receives between 45 and 55 percent of the
vote, a corresponding Competition Index score of .9 to 1.1 results.
Table 5.1 presents the index scores and party competition categories for various levels of Republican voter strength in elections.

As Figure 5.1 reveals, using the actual Republican vote compared
to the total presidential vote, the Republican "lock" on the South
that Black and Black and others have described is not quite as ap
parent, given the Democratic success in the 1992 and 1996 elections. Even in the absence of economic collapse or major scandal,
the loss of Republican support for the incumbent Republican president in four Southern states in 1992, states that had supported him
four years earlier, indicates that Republicans cannot automatically
count on all Southern states to support Republican candidates. Ob-
viously, the presence of third-party candidates greatly affects the index score. In reality, one data point, by definition, cannot be an

**Figure 5.1**
**Presidential Competition Score and Category, 1968–1996**

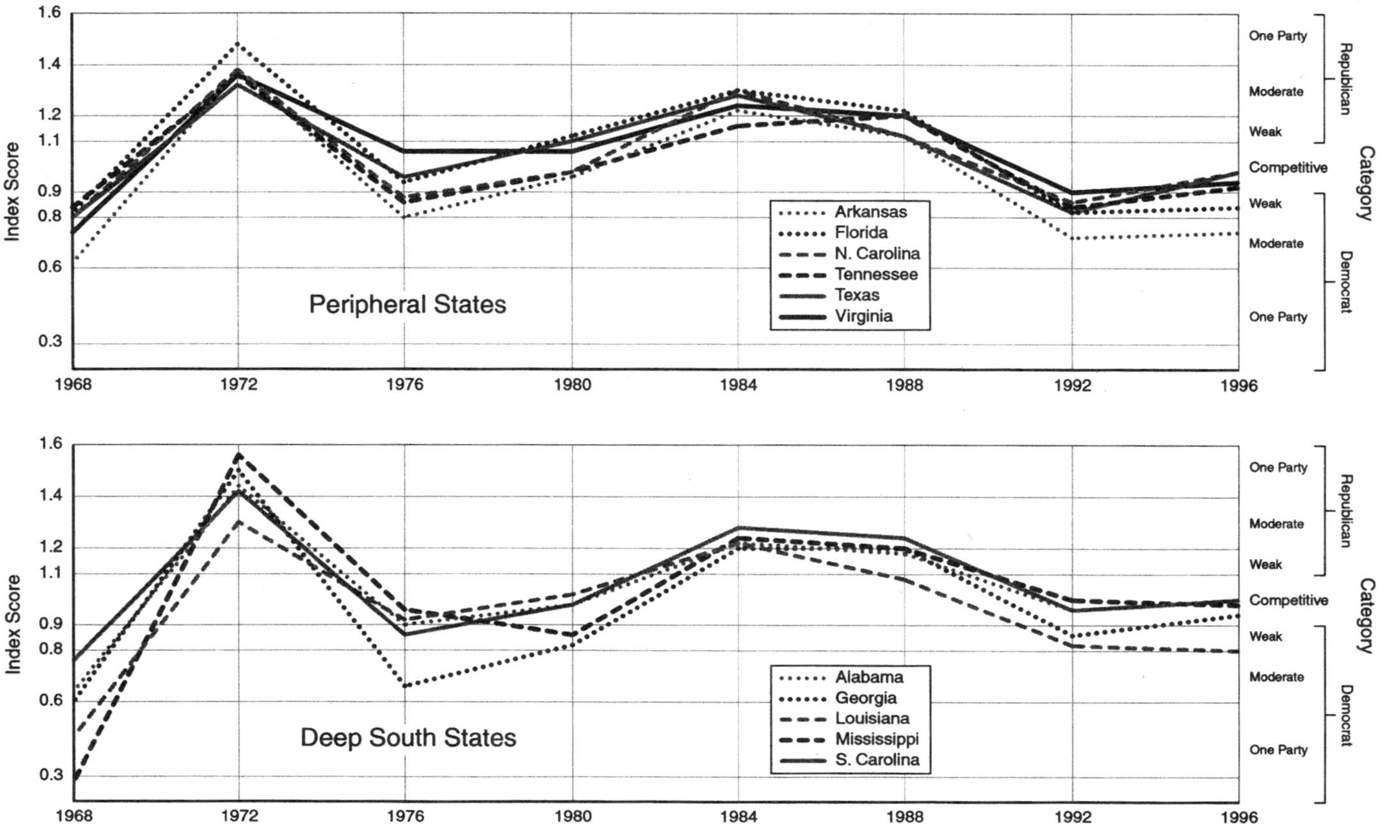

**Table 5.1**
**Party Competition Based on Composite B Index**

| Competitive Status | Index Score | Percent of Republican Vote |
|---|---|---|
| One-Party Republican | 2.0 to 1.4 | 70% or more |
| Modified One-Party Republican | 1.39 to 1.2 | 60 to 69% |
| Weak Republican | 1.19 to 1.11 | 56 to 59% |
| Competitive | 1.1 to .90 | 55 to 45% |
| Weak Democratic | .89 to .8 | 44 to 40% |
| Modified One-Party Democratic | 79 to .6 | 39 to 30% |
| One-Party Democratic | .59 to 0 | Less than 29% |

index score. The Competition scores presented in Figure 5.1 mask the fact that most of these states, regardless of the score and the competitive status category, were won by the Republican presidential candidate, which is why one might argue that Competition scores should be calculated solely on the two-party vote. However, what the scores and the competitive categories as presented in Figure 5.1 reveal is the competitive relationship between the two major parties in the context of these states at the presidential level.

Given the presence of third-party candidates in four of the eight elections (1968, 1980, 1992, and 1996), and *significant* third-party presence in three of those four (1968, 1992, and 1996), Southern voters are susceptible to switching support from candidate to candidate and party to party. However, it is not a foregone conclusion that voters who support third-party candidates will automatically support Republican candidates when no viable third-party candidate is running. For example, the 1996 Perot vote in Florida declined by half while the Democratic vote increased 9 percent and the Republican vote by only 1.4 percent. From 1992 to 1996, in five states—Arkansas, Alabama, Florida, Tennessee, and Louisiana—the Democrats' proportion of the two-party vote increased and increased by more than the Republican proportion of the vote. In five states—Mississippi, North Carolina, South Carolina, Texas, and Virginia—the Republican two-party vote increased more than the Democratic vote. In Georgia, the increases were the same for both parties. This suggests that given the right candidates and the right issues, either party can win Southern states at the presidential level and that the degree to which the Republican party has a lock on the South as argued by Black and Black may indeed be overstated.

As indicated previously, the presidential vote is subject to a broader array of factors, such as national and international issues, that may or may not reflect the strength of a political party more locally, especially within the confines of a particular state. By adopting David's Composite B Index, a better picture of politics within the states emerges. A Competition Index using the Republican vote for governor, U.S. senator, and statewide aggregation for U.S. House of Representatives candidates, as adapted from David (*Party*, 1972), for the eleven Southern states for the period 1968–1998 is presented in Figure 5.2. Both the Competition B Index scores and the corresponding competition categorization (summarized in Table 5.1) for Peripheral South states and Deep South states are presented for the same time period—1968–1998. The Republican vote for each office was totaled, divided by the total vote for all candidates for that office, and then multiplied by 2 to achieve the index score. In the event that a particular office was not elected in that year, an average of the preceding and following election results was used. Scores therefore range from 0.0 to 2.0.

Using this Composite B Index, states can be classified into traditional categories of competition. Defining "Competitive" as a candidate receiving between 45–55 percent of the vote in an election (Pfeiffer, 1967, p. 462), a Composite B Index of .9 to 1.1 reflects a Competitive situation in that state for the offices included. A 40—60 percent would result in a score of .8 to .89 or 1.11 to 1.2 and would be classified as a Weak Party state, whereas a One-Party state would reflect a vote of less than 30 percent or an index score of less than .59 or greater than 1.4.

The election of 1968 is used as a starting point for examining contemporary party competition because it is the first presidential election year following the adoption and implementation of the Voting Rights Act of 1965. The Voting Rights Act resulted in an increase in voter participation among African Americans and Hispanics in the South. For the first time in many places in the South, members of minority groups were able to freely register and vote. The 1964 Republican presidential candidate, Senator Barry Goldwater, focused attention on the Voting Rights act through his opposition to the act and his vote against it in the U.S. Senate. The 1964 presidential

# Figure 5.2
## Competition B Index Score and Category, 1968–1998
(based on Republican vote for Governor, U.S. Senator, and U.S. House candidate)

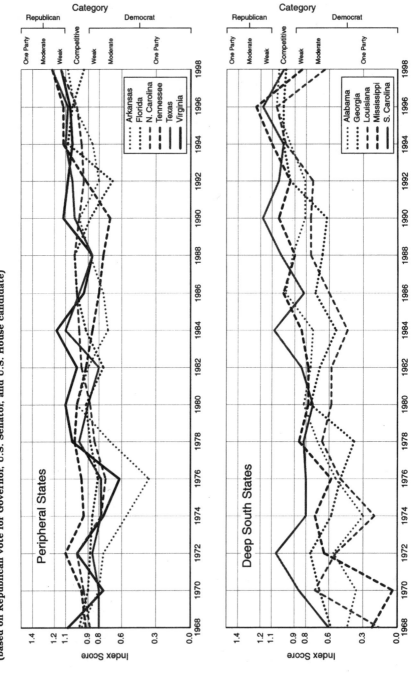

election solidified Black support for the Democratic party in the South. By 1968 the number of Black voters had increased as a result of the act and their support for the Democratic party was firmly established. The easier access to voting, the overall increase in the number of voters, and the overwhelming support from African American voters for Democratic candidates began the current transformation of Southern politics.

Examining the Composite B Index scores for Southern states since 1968, some clear trends emerge. Following the 1964 election, Peripheral South states resumed a Republican trend. The best Competitive position the Democratic party achieves in the post-Voting Rights Act period in Peripheral states is a brief period of One-Party Democratic status in Arkansas. Otherwise, a Competitive status dominates state party politics in the Peripheral South. North Carolina stands out as the most consistently Competitive state during this contemporary period. Virginia has exhibited the earliest flirtation with Weak Republican status, joined by Tennessee and Texas in the most recent series of elections. Arkansas remains the most Democratic bastion among the Peripheral South states. Clearly, the two parties are Competitive within the Peripheral South electorates for the most visible statewide and congressional elections.

After the 1998 election, the Republican party in the Peripheral South increased its Competitive status based on the strong showing of Republican governors in Texas and Tennessee, and the congressional races in North Carolina and Virginia. None of these states had a complete set of races for governor, senator, and House delegations, which limits the utility of the index for this particular year.

The most dramatic shifts have occurred among the Deep South states during this time period (see Figure 5.2). Although the Deep South states have been slower to relinquish their Democratic allegiance at the state level, by the end of the Reagan era, Mississippi, Alabama, and South Carolina were Competitive and Georgia and Louisiana had moved into a Modified Democratic category. By 1996, Georgia and Louisiana had joined Alabama in the Competitive category, while South Carolina reflected a Weak Republican status and Mississippi could be classified as a Modified One-Party Republican state. In 1998, with all Deep South states except Mississippi having elections for races other than the House, the Republican party was Competitive in most states. Louisiana remained on the Democratic side of the scale in the House and Senate elections in 1998, while Mississippi, which had only House elections in 1998, exhibited a stronger Democratic allegiance than it does with statewide races for Senate and governor. At the more grassroots level, the weakness of the Republican party is still present in some Deep South states.

As Havard (1972, p. 439) and Sundquist (1973, p. 257) found, the Republican increases in the 1964 presidential election and the resulting aftermath in the Deep South were due to alienated Democrats who generally returned to the Democratic party after Goldwater was gone. The one exception to this was South Carolina, where Senator Strom Thurmond's early switch to the Republican party established a base and a legitimacy for two-party growth (Cosman, *Five States*, 1967, p. 65). Although the Deep South states had resisted the move to two-party competition for offices other than the presidency after 1964, by 1996 and 1998 little difference existed between Peripheral and Deep South states at the sub-presidential statewide level, although Deep South states still appear to be weaker Republican territory. When long-term Democratic politicians retire or die, Deep South voters seem to be more likely to bring their non-presidential voting into alignment with their presidential voting behavior.

It can be argued that Composite B Index scores are still unduly influenced by national and even international issues and factors because many members of Congress are associated with these non-local issues through the nature of their activities in Washington. Although the core of congressional politics is to tend to local concerns through constituent relations or local projects (e.g., roads, military bases, etc.), non-local issues can still influence congressional election outcomes.

## GUBERNATORIAL COMPETITION

By calculating a standardized Competition score for gubernatorial races, as was done for the presidential elections previously, another picture of party competition within states emerges. The governorships is a quintessential localized state office that frequently reflects the unique character of a state's electorate and the issues that drive voters at that point in time.

Figure 5.3 presents the Competition scores for gubernatorial elections from 1967 to 1999 and the resulting competition status for the parties in the state. Among Peripheral South states, Virginia emerges as the most consistently Republican-leaning state with a pattern that has been very Competitive with movement in the direc-

**Figure 5.3**
**Gubernatorial Competition Score and Category, 1967–1999**

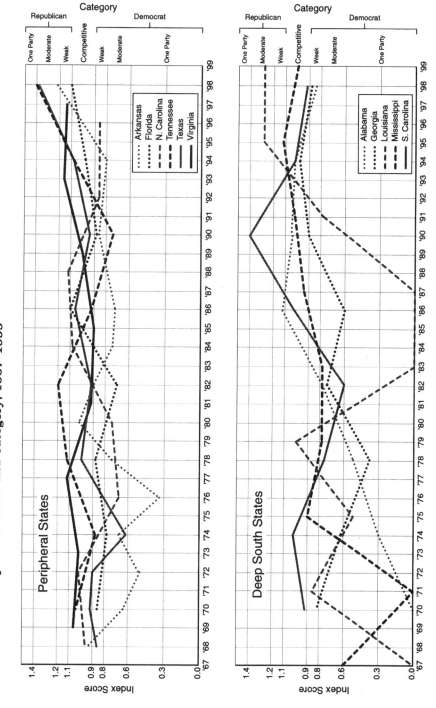

tion of Weak Republican status in gubernatorial elections throughout this period. Tennessee has alternated more widely between the
parties and their candidates, providing Democratic candidates with
strong wins, followed by a Republican strong win, and then inter-
spersed closer races. Texas has been the most consistently Competitive state at the gubernatorial level, whereas North Carolina and
Florida have been basically Competitive with a definite Democratic
tilt during this period. Arkansas remains the most consistently
Democratic Peripheral state, although it has elected a Republican
governor as well. Although the Republican party has been competitive in Virginia throughout this period, it was not competitive until
the 1970s in North Carolina, Tennessee, and Texas, and had to wait
until the 1980s in Florida and Arkansas.

Among Deep South states, South Carolina has been Competitive
throughout this period, having been a source of national Republican leaders who formulated and worked to implement the national
Republican party Southern strategy in the wake of the Goldwater
candidacy. Other Deep South states, however, did not emerge from
Democratic domination until the 1980s (Alabama and Mississippi)
and 1990 (Georgia). Louisiana elected a Republican governor as
early as 1979, but waited until 1995 to repeat a Republican gubernatorial victory as a result of a bitter split in the Democratic primary
and a run-off election laced with racial overtones. Georgia has remained the most Democratic state in that it has not elected a Republican governor in contemporary times. The reality, though, is
that every Southern state has become Competitive at the gubernatorial level in that either major party is in a position to elect a governor given the right candidate and circumstances.

## STATE LEGISLATIVE COMPETITION

Finally, a brief look at party Competitive status in state legislative
seats provides the most local-level picture of party strength
throughout an entire state. The state legislature, especially in
Southern states where governors have traditionally had very cir-
cumspect powers subject to legislative oversight, is a particularly
important arena in which to gauge Republican electoral success.
Historically, the number of Republicans elected to state legislative
seats in the South has been minimal. The overwhelming number of
state legislative seats won by Republicans in the South has been in
urban districts—a further limitation of Republican presence as the

South has been the nation's least urban region. The hometowns of Republican state legislators read like a list of the South's large cities with an occasional "mountain" town appearing here and there (*Book of the States*).

Further, the state legislative level is a potentially critical level for political party success and growth because of the control that state legislators exercise over redistricting. Redistricting becomes especially important in the presence of the Supreme Court's seeming retreat from "one man, one vote" rulings concerning state reapportionment, the Court's changing position on majority-minority districts, and the decennial census. Control of the state legislature can assist a political party in keeping control of elective offices, although not always. As stated previously, when the Department of Justice insisted on the creation of more majority-minority districts for legislative bodies, Democrats saw their number of seats decline, especially in Congress, with the concentration of strongly Democratic minority voters in a few districts and the shift of White voters away from the Democratic party. Control of the state legislature will nevertheless be important for the next decade in the wake of the 2000 Census and the gain in congressional seats that is anticipated in some Southern states.

To measure the competitive position of the parties at the state legislative level in the absence of statewide vote totals for candidates by party, a Lag Score has been developed. To calculate the Lag Score, the number of seats held by the Republicans in both houses of the state legislature were totaled. Taking the percentage of the vote for governor in the last election and multiplying it times the total number of seats available in the legislative chambers results in the number of seats the party should hold if they had received the same proportion of the vote for legislative seats as they did for governor. The vote for governor is used because the governor is the best statewide office to reflect broader party strength in the state and is an office focused on the same breadth of state issues that legislators also have to wrestle with. Dividing the number of seats the Republican party should have (based on the vote for governor) into the number of seats actually held by the party provides a measure of whether and to what degree the legislative party lags behind the gubernatorial party in the state.

The Lag Score (see Figure 5.4) represents the proportion of legislative seats held compared to what the Republican party should have if they were as successful as their candidate for governor. For

**Figure 5.4**
**State Legislative Lag Score**

$$\text{Lag Score} = \frac{\#L}{\%\text{gvote}}$$

%gvote = total number of state legislative seats multiplied by the percentage of the vote for the Republican governor preceding election

#L = actual number of seats in state legislature held by Republicans

example, a Lag Score of .75 means that the Republican party holds only three-fourths of the seats in the state legislature that they should hold if they received the same proportion of the vote as the governor in the last election. The actual number of seats held by the party may change from year to year, but the Lag Score adjusts to reflect the party fortunes compared to the success of electing a governor. So the number of seats could remain constant and the Lag Score could increase if the party's gubernatorial candidate did not run well in the last election, thereby indicating that the legislative party had done better in holding its relative position than the party did statewide. Again, since the party's success is being anchored to the election for one office—the governor—the Lag Score is only a limited indicator of party strength; however, the state legislator remains the most local reflection of party preference among voters for an office that handles broad policy issues for the entire state. Therefore, the governor and the state legislature are bound much like the president and Congress in general voter perception. State legislators, similar to members of Congress, benefit from a local familiarity and from a strong incumbent advantage not enjoyed by presidents or governors. Because state legislators are elected from small, homogeneous districts, a political party's long-term success rests ultimately at this grassroots level.

Figure 5.5 presents the Lag Score and the corresponding Competitive categories for the 1968–1999 time period. The most immediate impression from the chart is the overwhelming Democratic dominance throughout most of this contemporary period. Tennessee and Florida are the only states to exhibit a noticeable Republican presence. The Mountain Republican presence in Tennessee and North Carolina has provided at least a modicum of GOP representation throughout the latter part of the twentieth century. Coupled

**Figure 5.5**
**State Legislative Lag Score and Category, 1968–1999**

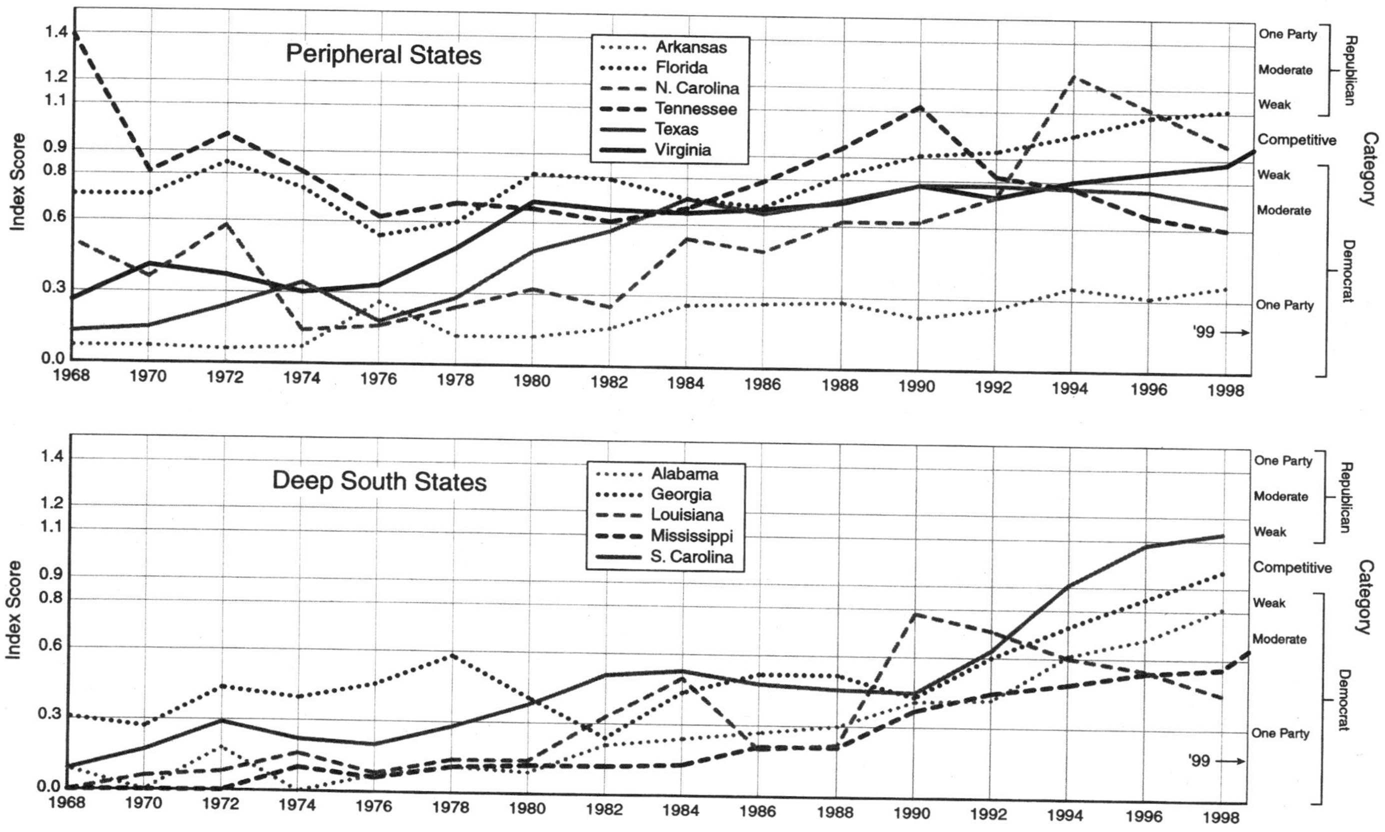

with urban Republicanism noted by Key and others, these three Peripheral states have exhibited the most consistent pattern of Republican party representation, but it was not until 1988 that Tennessee finally achieved a Competitive status at the state legislative level, followed by Florida in 1990. However, the 1994 Republican Revolution that captured control of Congress had a smaller impact at the state legislative level. North Carolina moved into a situation where Republicans were over-represented in the legislature compared to their performance at the gubernatorial level, but the GOP actually lost competitive ground in Tennessee and Texas.

In the Deep South, every state has shown increased Republican presence, but not until 1994 in South Carolina did a Deep South state reach a Competitive status in the state legislature. Only in Georgia among other Deep South states is the Republican party close to the performance they have attained at the gubernatorial level. In terms of the patterns, Arkansas more closely resembles the Deep South at the legislative level than its Peripheral South sisters. All of these states started with virtually no Republican legislative presence and have progressed to a point where Republicans hold two-thirds to three-fourths of the seats they should hold based on how well their gubernatorial candidates have done. On the other hand, among Deep South states South Carolina has moved very quickly to resemble the position of the Republican party in most Peripheral states, and has moved to a position where Republicans in the state legislature are doing better than their gubernatorial candidates. The fact that, on average, 80 percent of legislative incumbents win re-election further makes the Republican challenge to reach parity difficult. At this basic level where candidates are first identified for other statewide and national offices, the Republican party overall still lags substantially behind its Democratic counterpart.

The shallow upward trends during most of this period confirm the gradual improvement in the level of competition for the Republican party at the state legislative level in the Peripheral states. The relative position of a state may vary from year to year in the ebb and flow of electoral campaigns, but North Carolina and Arkansas remain the most consistently Democratic states in the Peripheral South, while the other four continue a gradual movement in the direction of the Republican party.

The steeper trends for the Deep South states toward the upper right on Figure 5.5 demonstrate the more rapid movement in the

Deep South states toward the Republican party compared to the Peripheral South. Georgia, Alabama, and Louisiana remain the most Democratic states in the Deep South, although they are clustered in the Competitive range. South Carolina and Mississippi exhibit the earliest and most consistent presence of Republican party support during this period.

In relation to Competitive status between the parties in the South, among Peripheral South states, 1972 witnessed their return to the Republican fold at the presidential level and at the gubernatorial and congressional levels in half of the states. In the others, the 1980s ushered in competition at the gubernatorial and congressional levels. State legislative competition has finally emerged in all but one of the Peripheral states, but in Arkansas in particular, and also in Tennessee and Texas, the Republican party lags far behind its gubernatorial candidates and the Democrats in electing its members to office.

In the Deep South, it was not until 1972 that these states established a Republican trend at the presidential level, and not until the 1980s that they began to successfully compete at the gubernatorial and congressional levels. South Carolina stands alone as a Competitive state that leans Republican at the state legislative level, and Georgia has moved into the Competitive category. Although Alabama continues to move toward a Competitive status, Mississippi and Louisiana are still waiting for Competitive status at the state legislative level.

*Chapter 6*

# Party Competition in the South

What, then, does all of this add up to? What has occurred to transform the South from a Democratic bastion to a competitive two-party region? And what does the future hold for the parties given the current trends?

In general, there is much evidence that the South is increasingly approximating the remainder of the country politically and socially—the Republican party now wins elections in the South with regularity, voters will publicly identify themselves as Republicans, registration and voting rates resemble those in the rest of the nation, income and educational attainment are moving closer to national norms. Differences also persist—the South is more Republican than the rest of the country in national elections, it remains more conservative on many social issues, and it does still lag behind in overall income and educational measures.

In terms of the most visible national elections—presidential elections—the South is still considered to be essential by Republicans if they are to win the White House and control of Congress. As recently as 1992, Black and Black argued that the region was the "Vital South." More recently, though, Eamon argues that "the South is central to American politics but rarely determines the winner in presidential elections" (1997, p. 129). As Table 2.2 indicates, only three times has the South made a difference in winning or losing the

White House for either major party. "Looking at the United States as a whole, the 1992 election proves conclusively that the non-Southern megastates remain a powerful force in the 1990s. As in 1952 and 1960, a substantial victory in the megastates provides the most direct route to the White House" (Eamon, 1997, p. 128).

Eamon defines the six non-Southern megastates as New York, Pennsylvania, Ohio, Illinois, Michigan, and California. These states are the largest states based on population; they have very diverse populations; are overwhelmingly urban; have large media markets; and possess two-thirds, or 171, of the electoral votes needed to win the presidency. In contrast, the Deep South contains 46 electoral votes; the Peripheral South, 44 electoral votes; and Texas/Florida, 57 electoral votes, for a total of 147 electoral votes spread across eleven states. The mathematics suggest that on a national level, concentrating resources on the megastates is more useful than concentrating on the South as a region.

The most recent elections also support the notion that the South cannot be counted on to vote as a region, having split its votes between the two major party candidates in both elections in 1992 and 1996. Further, Eamon separates Texas and Florida from the remainder of the South because they are now megastates. Although Eamon makes a convincing argument for presidential candidates to develop a megastate strategy to win the White House, it is also the case that the megastates do not always vote as a bloc either. Clinton, a native Southerner, lost the South but carried all of the non-Southern megastates in 1992 and 1996, plus Florida in 1996. Even with the argument that the South is not essential at the presidential level, the two megastates in the South—Florida and Texas—did not support the Democratic candidate in 1992, and only one did in 1996, whereas the other megastates all supported the Democratic candidate in both elections—the regional difference persists even here.

In non-presidential elections, the South continues to play a large regional role, especially in Congress where the influence of Southern members continues to shape the national agenda in terms of both priorities and policies that grow from the historic experience of the region and its people. Despite the pressures that have pushed the South to more closely approximate the remainder of the country, several historical factors continue to strongly influence the changes that have spread across the South and to shape its regional distinctiveness.

## RACE

"Amid overall growth, the South's population mix has shifted: Whites down from 76 percent in the mid-1970s to 68 percent; Blacks gaining from 18 percent to 19 percent; and Hispanics jumping from five percent to 11 percent over a 20–year period" (*State of the South*, 1998, p. 6). At the same time, the size of the middle class in the South has grown among all racial and ethnic groups. "As family income rises, dollars are becoming more concentrated in the hands of the South's highest income White, Black and Hispanic families" (*State of the South*, 1998, p. 20). The political implications of these demographic changes grow from the partisan shifts that have been occurring since the New Deal era in the South.

The Democratic party's political dominance of the South was rooted in the Civil War and the struggle over slavery. As long as Blacks were denied access to the ballot across the South, Democratic hegemony persisted. The backbone of Southern Republicanism in many parts of the South was the handful of Blacks who were allowed to vote, coupled with pockets of White Mountain Republicans and later urban immigrants who brought their Republicanism with them from other parts of the country. Not until 1964 did most Blacks in the South shift their allegiance to the Democratic party, making it possible for Johnson to carry some Peripheral South states that otherwise would have joined their Deep South cousins in support of the Republican presidential candidate. It was not until 1968 that a large number of Blacks registered and voted, enabling them to become a more determining factor in Southern states. In the three years following passage of the Voting Rights Act, the proportion of Blacks who were registered to vote rose to over half of those eligible (Scher, 1997, p. 250). In direct response to the removal of barriers to registration that had kept many poor people from voting and the increased perception that Blacks might "take over," the proportion of White voters increased as well.

At the same time that Blacks were registering and voting in much higher numbers than previously, Richard Nixon was successfully pursuing the Republican nomination and the presidency on an overt Southern strategy of courting White voters who had supported Goldwater in 1964 and George Wallace in 1968. As a result, Black voters moved even more heavily into the Democratic party.

The increase in Black participation within the Democratic party resulted in White Democratic candidates who actively sought the support of African American voters through espousing positions that were more liberal or progressive than many of the White Democratic voters were prepared to support. As a result, the Democrats began to nominate candidates that a large proportion of White Democrats found farther removed from their positions than the Republican candidates who were actively courting them with traditionally conservative Democratic positions and issues and only lightly veiled race-anchored appeals. The Southern strategy to win over White voters to the Republican party was being helped by the increased involvement of Blacks in the Democratic party in primary and general elections.

Although African American turnout in elections continues to be about 10 percentage points below White turnout, the impact of African American voters witnessed the eventual solicitation of Black voters by such long-time segregationist Democratic politicians as George Wallace and John Stennis. The 10 percent lower turnout rates and the continuing 10 percent gap between the proportion of African Americans and Whites registered to vote, makes it more difficult for contemporary Democratic candidates to win election. Nearly 65 percent of Southern White voters in the 1990s voted for Republican candidates even if they hadn't formally changed their political party identification. Only three Southern states have formal party registration—North Carolina, Louisiana, and Florida.

As Black and Black have pointed out, Democratic candidates have to carry approximately 40 percent of the White vote and 85 percent of the Black vote to have a chance to win election in most of the South (*Vital South,* 1992). In 1996, Clinton carried 43 percent of the White vote nationally and 84 percent of the Black vote to win. In the South, he carried little more than a third of the White vote, 87 percent of the Black vote, and almost 75 percent of the Hispanic vote to carry four states—Arkansas, Florida, Louisiana, and Tennessee.

With national trends that have prevailed throughout the latter half of the twentieth century, voters with lower levels of education and wealth have tended to vote for Democratic rather than Republican candidates. In the South, fewer skilled workers have had to move to find jobs. Among the fastest growing segment of the population—Hispanics—40 percent of adult Hispanics who have moved to the South from within the United States between 1970 and 1997 had less than a high school education. "Among all adult domestic in-migrants, the South attracted 31 percent with just a high school diploma and 14 percent with less than a high school education"

(*State of the South*, 1998, p. 8). During this same time period—1990 to 1997—African American in-migration reached historic highs—65 percent of the nation's African American population growth occurred in the South, and the region contained 46 percent of the nation's total growth (*State of the South*, 1998, p. 8). The influx of less educated and minority people to the South may have offset some of the growth in Republican identification among the growing higher income, better educated population in the South.

At the congressional level the influence of race has resulted in dramatic changes as well. The Southern Strategy has trickled down from the presidential level to the state level as the Republican party has tried to tie Senate and House races to the presidential candidates (Beachler, 1996, p. 779). The federal courts have further contributed to the movement of Whites out of the Democratic party by insisting on the creation of more majority-minority districts. In the wake of the 1980 and the 1990 Census redistricting, state legislatures (that were still heavily controlled by Democrats) were able to draw congressional and legislative districts that maximized partisan divisions. By splitting strongly White Republican areas among White and Black Democratic voters, or by concentrating strong Republican areas into a single district, Democrats continued to dominate legislative elections, especially in rural areas. Because the Department of Justice required more African American and Hispanic voters to be concentrated into single districts in order to ensure the election of Black and Hispanic representatives, the remaining White Democrats were often submerged in a sea of White Republicans.

Following redistricting, the 1992 election did have the intended effect of increasing the number of African Americans in the House from 25 to 38. In the South the number of African Americans rose from 5 to 17. An additional result was the creation of 21 more strongly Republican districts and 10 more strongly Democratic districts. As Democratic candidates recognized the changes occurring through redistricting and voter allegiance, retirements increased. By 1994 the Republicans won a majority of the congressional seats in the South for the first time since Reconstruction. In 1995 five White Southern Democrats switched to the Republican party in the middle of their terms. In 1996 Republicans continued to gain congressional seats in every Southern state except North Carolina where they lost seats. That year Republicans held almost 57 percent of Southern congressional seats. In states with high minority popu-

lations, the 1996 election resulted in only eleven Democratic representatives winning House seats. In each of four Deep South
states—Alabama, Mississippi, South Carolina, and Louisiana—one
White Democrat and one Black Democrat were elected to Congress.
In the state of Georgia three Black Democrats and no White Democrats were elected. Seven of the eleven Democratic representatives
in the House from the Deep South were Black. Between 1990 and
1998, the parties in the South had essentially reversed positions in
the proportion of House seats they controlled.

Whereas nationally the Republican party had traditionally relied
upon the Midwest for most of its congressional strength, in the
1990s it began to rely heavily on the South. Going into the 1998
election, most of the congressional leadership for the Republican
party came from Southern states—for example, House Speaker
Newt Gingrich (GA), House Majority Leader Dick Armey (TX), House
Whip Tom DeLay (TX), and Senate Majority Leader Trent Lott (MS).
When Newt Gingrich stepped down as Speaker of the House, his heir
apparent was Bob Livingston from Louisiana until his resignation at
the revelation of an earlier extramarital affair. Republicans finally
elected Midwesterner Dennis Hastert of Illinois as their new
Speaker.

Congressional leadership is important for a political party nationally, because the leaders in the Senate and House set the agenda for
consideration of laws, regulations, and taxes. In terms of organizing
committees in Congress—the units in which most of the work of
Congress is done—the congressional leadership appoints membership and leadership of key committees. The Republican House majority rests upon the strong advantage that they hold in the
Southern state delegations; for example, after the 1992 election
29.5 percent of the House seats came from the South; after the 1996
election, 31 percent; and after the 1998 election, 32 percent came
from the South. Similarly, after 1992, 29 percent of the Republican
House seats were from the East, but after 1996, Republican seats
from the East had declined to only 17 percent of the Republican total. The Democrats, however, have shifted from a reliance on the
South to a reliance on the Northeastern states for congressional
election success. Since 1962, the Northeast region has become increasingly Democratic, including 1998.

In 1997, the federal courts struck down the majority-minority redistricting that appeared to have presaged the Republican party legislative growth. Race has been declared as *not* a sole acceptable

basis for drawing districts. Therefore, as state legislatures search for other criteria on which to redraw districts, the opportunity to create districts more friendly to Democratic candidates arises. If the percentage of African Americans and Hispanics in current majority-minority districts were reduced and these voters shifted to other districts, Democrats might have better opportunities to regain some seats that they lost in the mid-1990s. Republican ascendance in the South at the congressional level may have peaked. The creation of safe or heavily Republican districts has been exhausted through Democratic efforts to concentrate Republican voters in particular districts and through the earlier court requirements to create majority-minority districts. Weaker support for Republican candidates among younger voters in 1992 and 1996, and redistricting in response to the court's striking down majority-minority districts in 1996–1997, should bear witness to a resurgence of the Democratic congressional presence in the twenty-first century that would result in a more balanced two-party congressional outcome in the South.

Race continues to be a dominant force in Southern elections. The political parties have essentially switched positions during the last half of the twentieth century in terms of the allegiance of White voters, their positions on many issues, and their control of political office. In large measure, the Civil Rights movement and the attendant legislative and judicial initiatives have transformed the political landscape of the South. However, the Democratic party is still competitive across the South, attesting to the success of the Civil Rights movement. It is ironic that because African Americans have become substantially more politically involved since the late 1960s, the Democratic party has been saved from assuming the truly weak position of the Republican party in the South in the first half of the century. The Democratic party's dominance in the first half of the twentieth century rested heavily on keeping Blacks out of the political, social, and economic mainstream. In the latter half of the century, it has been Black political participation that has kept the Democratic party as competitive as it has been with the Republican party in the South. Race has been a prime factor in the partisan realignment of the South. "The old black/white divisions are still stuck in the core of the region even as new immigrants are rapidly creating a multiracial, multi-ethnic South" (*State of the South*, 1998, p. 4).

## GENDER

The emergence of the Gender Gap in the 1980s has also had an impact in the South. Just as the Civil Rights movement transformed participation for Blacks and Whites in the South, the Women's Movement has transformed the role models for women in the South. Women now constitute 52 percent of the electorate nationally. Among all voters, Democrats nationally received 8 percent more of women's votes than Republicans in 1996. In 1996, the Republican presidential candidate, Bob Dole, received 44 percent of the male vote compared to 43 percent for Democrat Bill Clinton; among women the Republican candidate received only 38 percent compared to the Democrat's 54 percent. Women showed a clear preference for the Democrats in 1996. Democrats increased their 1996 percentage of the male vote by 2 percentage points over the proportion obtained in 1992. The Democratic increase in 1996 among women was 9 percent over 1992. Between 1992 and 1996, Republicans at the national level witnessed a decline in support among women, and a more even split among men.

In seven of the Southern states (see Table 6.1), over 50 percent of the male vote went to the Republican presidential candidate in 1996, and the Republicans carried all seven states. In the four states carried by the Democratic candidate, males provided half or fewer of their votes to the Republicans. In no Southern state did a majority of female voters support the Republican candidate.

Although a strategy by the Democrats to appeal to women voters has provided positive results for the party, the success of the Republican party and its candidates in appealing to males, particularly White male voters, has proven to be even more successful in the South. A gender gap exists in every Southern state in varying degrees with female voters stronger in their support of the Democratic party, and men more supportive of the Republican party. In the South in 1996, only 36 percent of White voters voted for Clinton compared to 56 percent for Dole. Although it was a 2 percent increase over 1992 for the Democrats, it was not sufficient to ensure electoral success at the presidential level in most Southern states, nor for other offices in Southern states in 1996 (*America at the Polls*, 1996, p. 14).

## RELIGION

Religion continues to play a strong role in Southern politics, perhaps more so now than in the past. Although the South historically

**Table 6.1**
**Gender Differences, 1992–1996**

|  | Gender Difference in Republican Support |  | Dole | Clinton | Perot |
|---|---|---|---|---|---|
| NATIONAL |  |  | 49% | 41% | 8% |
|  |  | Men | 44% | 43% | 10% |
|  |  | Women | 38% | 54% | 7% |
| PERIPHERAL |  |  |  |  |  |
| Arkansas | -9% | Men | 44% | 47% | 6% |
|  |  | Women | 35% | 59% | 5% |
| Florida | -8% | Men | 46% | 41% | 11% |
|  |  | Women | 38% | 54% | 8% |
| N. Carolina | -7% | Men | 53% | 38% | 8% |
|  |  | Women | 46% | 49% | 5% |
| Tennessee | -8% | Men | 50% | 42% | 7% |
|  |  | Women | 42% | 53% | 5% |
| Texas | -7% | Men | 53% | 39% | 7% |
|  |  | Women | 46% | 49% | 5% |
| Virginia | -9% | Men | 52% | 39% | 7% |
|  |  | Women | 43% | 49% | 6% |
|  |  |  |  |  |  |
| DEEP |  |  |  |  |  |
| Alabama | -5% | Men | 53% | 37% | 7% |
|  |  | Women | 48% | 46% | 5% |
| Georgia | -13% | Men | 54% | 39% | 7% |
|  |  | Women | 41% | 52% | 6% |
| Louisiana | -7% | Men | 44% | 46% | 9% |
|  |  | Women | 37% | 57% | 6% |
| Mississippi | -10% | Men | 58% | 37% | 5% |
|  |  | Women | 48% | 48% | 4% |
| S. Carolina | -4% | Men | 52% | 41% | 6% |
|  |  | Women | 48% | 46% | 5% |

Source: *America at the Polls*, 1996

was the leader in church attendance and church membership, political activity was fairly carefully isolated from religion (except for the fact that belonging to a church, or at least being able to quote scripture, was an essential part of most successful Southern politicians).

Historically, Protestantism has been the dominant religious tradition in the South both among Whites and Blacks. Given the high levels of poverty and lack of economic opportunity in the South, religion became one of the social institutions where poor people could participate and the promise of a better life was presented. With both Blacks and poor Whites excluded from most other social organizations that typically provided social cohesion and introduction to community life and values—schools, many jobs and occupations, civic organizations, and political parties—during much of the twentieth century, churches and religion became a primary means of connection to others outside the family. In most parts of the United States, political parties played an active role in socializing citizens. "But virtually none of this was true of the factional system of old style southern Democratic politics. Indeed, the emphasis was on keeping people out of politics, not on making them feel a part of the system" (Scher, 1997, p. 64).

During most of this century, churches focused the attention of their parishioners on the "other" world. Just as political parties resisted the inclusion of very many people, churches tried to maximize inclusion by focusing attention not on the problems of the temporal world, but on the promise of a better life in the next world. In the South, the role of the churches in social control has been strong. Southern churches reinforced the social order and the dominant racial and social policies of the White elite. It is not an accident that churches are one of the most segregated institutions in the South.

The fact that people in the South were not encouraged by Democrats to be active in political parties may ultimately have been a factor contributing to the departure of many voters from the Democratic party. As the dominant Democratic party was perceived as departing from the values of the prevailing social order by embracing "liberal" positions and welcoming Blacks, there was more impetus for conservative Christians to become more active politically. With little opposition from traditional Republican party members, it was relatively simple for the increasingly politically active conservative Christians to exercise influence quickly within the minority Republican party in the South. In a departure from the past, White Protestant ministers began to exhort their members to become politically active in order to restore moral authority to the social environment. Thus, by the late 1990s, Guth could write that the Christian Coalition conservatives were the single largest identifiable group within the Republican party (1993, p. 172).

The melding together of religion and politics was not totally unprecedented, however. Black ministers were in the forefront of the Civil Rights movement, providing encouragement from the pulpit for their members to become socially and politically active, endorsing

political candidates, and in some instances running for office themselves. The emergence of these same behaviors among White Protestants was almost a natural reaction to offset the successes they
observed among Black religious leaders who were often perceived by
some to be a threat to the basic social order.

Just as Black churches conducted voter registration drives during the Civil Rights period, White churches began to do the same in
the latter third of the twentieth century. As a result, the number of
African American voters increased as did the number of Whites, off-
setting some of the anticipated increase in minority political
strength envisioned as an outcome of the Voting Rights Act in 1965.

Whereas nationally the overall Protestant vote split 50 percent for
Dole and 41 percent for Clinton, White Protestants voted 53 percent
Republican and only 36 percent Democratic. Because most Whites
in the South are Protestant, and as the authors in Bullock and Rozell (*The New Politics*, 1998) point out, conservative Christian Protestants are the bedrock of the Republican party in states across the
South, Southern White voters split even more heavily for the Republican presidential candidate in 1996—56 percent Republican to 36
percent for the Democrats. At the same time, the vast majority of African Americans are also Protestants and cast over 80 percent of
their votes for the Democratic party in 1996. The overwhelming support of African Americans for the Democratic party candidate kept
the Protestant vote for the two major parties competitive. In 1996,
each of the other categories of religious preference—Catholic (53
percent), Jewish (78 percent), members of other religions (60 percent), and those with no religious preference (59 percent)—cast a
majority of their votes for the Democrats, whereas half of the Protestant vote (50 percent) went for the Republican candidate (*America at
the Polls*, 1996, p. 14).

## SUMMARY

From a political standpoint, the three factors of race, gender, and
religion continue to play a pivotal role in Southern politics. The conservative, White-male dominated, individualistic, moralistic foundation that was the traditional bedrock of the Democratic
party—the foundation that allowed the party to dominate politics
from Reconstruction until the middle of the twentieth century—still
persists in the South today. Perhaps it is not quite as strong or as
controlling as it once was because of the influx of non-Southerners

to the region, the incredible turmoil of the 1960s and 1970s, and the pervasive presence of the media-dispersed national culture, but it persists nevertheless. Without doubt, the Democratic party in its ascendancy was a conservative, White, male entity. As the Democratic party pursued policies and positions that undermined or challenged the continuing dominance of conservative White males, these identifiers began to leave the party. The party of the conservative White male is now the Republican party, particularly in the South.

In 1949, V. O. Key set the tone and defined the ensuing fifty years of study of the South and its politics. In addition, he defined political realignment for political researchers. He focused on the reasons for large groups of voters to shift their partisan allegiances from one political party to another. For Key a partisan realignment required (1) deeply concerned voters, (2) a relatively high degree of electoral involvement, (3) voting results that revealed sharp alteration of pre-existing cleavages within the electorate, and (4) persistence of the electoral shift over time. In addition, he originally saw a catastrophic event of some sort that would cause the electoral shift to occur—frequently referred to as a critical election.

By briefly examining each of Key's realignment characteristics, an understanding of whether a partisan realignment has occurred in the South should be easier to determine. Key argued that a group of concerned voters was the first pre-requisite for realignment. In the South, two groups of concerned voters can be identified—African Americans and conservative Whites. African Americans entered the ranks of voters in the latter half of the twentieth century after a long struggle to win access to the ballot. Prior to the 1960s, those Blacks who could vote aligned themselves primarily with the Republican party in the South. Following the Voting Rights Act and the expansion of Black voters that ensued, allegiance among Black voters shifted heavily to the Democratic party because it was perceived, at least at the national level, as championing the cause of Black voter registration and participation. At the same time, White voters in the South who had been strong supporters of the Democratic party when it resisted Black participation in politics and social life, began to shift their allegiance to the Republican party as it more actively positioned itself in opposition to many of the Democratic positions on social and economic issues. In addition, the rise of political activism among conservative Christians further supported the movement of many Whites toward the Republican party as the better alternative for preserving traditional cultural values (Black and Black, *Politics and Society*, 1987; Scher, 1997). There is evidence, then, to support Key's first pre-requisite—the existence in the South in the latter part of the century of groups of deeply concerned voters.

Second, Key looks for relatively high degrees of electoral involvement. An anticipated outcome of the Civil Rights era legislation, and the 1965 Voting Rights Act in particular, was the increase in the number of voters in the South, both Black and White; however, electoral participation has not increased overall.

Midterm, or non-presidential, election years are an indicator of the level of electoral participation by the most committed partisan voters. Whereas presidential elections typically prompt the highest levels of voter participation in elections—averaging approximately 50 percent since 1976—in midterm elections when there is no presidential election, only 40 percent of the eligible voters on average are likely to participate. Since a high point in 1966 when 49 percent of voters voted in the midterm election, participation has seemingly stabilized at a lower level—1986 and 1990 attracted only 36 percent of the eligible voters, 1994 "jumped" to 38.8 percent, and 1998 resulted in 38 percent of eligible voters participating.

Registering to vote, which is necessary before one can vote in either a primary or general election, provides another indication of electoral involvement. Prior to the Voting Rights Act of 1965, it is estimated that only 10 percent of Blacks eligible to vote were registered. In 1968, three years after the Voting Rights Act was passed, approximately 60 percent of eligible Blacks were registered (Scher, 1997, pp. 250–251). Since that time, African American registration has lagged approximately 10 percentage points behind White registration. The percentage of eligible voters registered declined after 1972 with the addition of 18- to 20-year-old voters who have historically had the worst voter registration and participation rates of any age group. Turnout rates, the percentage of registered voters who actually vote in an election, also reflect approximately a 10 percentage point lag between White voters and Black voters (Scher, 1997, p. 251).

Part of the Democratic success at the presidential level in 1996 may have been due to the fact that both the gap in voter registration and voting narrowed according to the U.S. Bureau of the Census. In the 1996 election, 67.7 percent of Whites and 63.5 percent of African Americans indicated that they were registered to vote, while 56 percent of Whites and 50.6 percent of African Americans reported voting. Even though self-reporting tends to inflate the percentages somewhat, the gap between the political participation rates of Whites and African Americans appears to be closing, which may limit the ability of the Republican party to continue its growth in the South or nationally (U.S. Bureau of the Census, "Percent Reported Voted," 1997).

Although both voter registration and turnout by race are estimates because voter records do not record and report race, the evidence suggests that the degree of voter involvement is changing in the South. Historically, political participation has been lowest in the South compared to other regions of the country. In the last four presidential elections, the level of voter registration in the South has trailed only the Midwest, and although voting participation has continued to lag, in 1992 and 1996 voting rates in the South as a region surpassed the West. In non-presidential elections, Southern rates of voting continue to fall behind other regions of the country (U.S. Bureau of the Census, "Percent Reported Voted," 1997).

However, Key only required a "relatively" high degree of involvement. The period from 1968 to the present in the South does reflect greater participation among both African Americans and Whites than previous to the passage of the Voting Rights Act; relatively speaking, involvement has increased.

Third, Key required voting results that revealed sharp alteration of pre-existing cleavages within the electorate. It could be argued that the very entrance of large numbers of non-Southerners into the South and the inclusion of Blacks as political participants, created cleavages that did not exist before. It was not so much that pre-existing cleavages changed, but rather that cleavages that were not there before emerged in a forceful manner as the basic electorate expanded and changed. The adoption of a strong civil rights stance by the national Democratic party with the accession of Lyndon Johnson to the presidency in 1963 and his election in 1964, the entry of large numbers of Blacks into the electorate following the 1965 Voting Rights Act, and the active pursuit of Southern White voters by the national Republican party beginning with Goldwater in 1964 and continuing with more success during the Nixon presidency (1968–1974), created a sharp alteration of pre-existing cleavages in the South.

As discussed previously, race was a major source of cleavage during most of the early twentieth century in the South. White Democrats maintained a political system that excluded most Blacks.

Those Blacks who did participate in the political arena tended to be Republicans—a legacy of the Civil War and Reconstruction. By the 1960s nationally, and the 1970s and 1980s within Southern states, a majority of Southern Whites shifted their partisan allegiance to the Republican party, and an overwhelming majority of Blacks shifted their allegiance to the Democratic party. The changes within the Democratic and Republican parties prompted the movement of primary constituencies—Black and White—to abandon their previous party identification for the other major party, or for an independent status. Within the South, the evidence supports the sharp shift in partisan cleavages during the latter half of the twentieth century that Key had required.

Finally, Key required that the electoral shift persist over time. In the South, the alteration in electoral behavior has persisted for several elections. Clearly, the persistence has been most sustained at the presidential level; however, the shift to the Republican party continues to trickle down to congressional, statewide, and state legislative races. Although Republicans have lost the last two presidential elections nationally, and approximately a third of the South's electoral votes have been won by the Democratic candidate in 1992 and 1996, the Republican party holds a majority of Southern governorships, U.S. Senate seats, and House of Representatives seats. By most measures, the South is no longer a one-party region, nor is any single state in the South a one-party state. Republican voting trends have persisted long enough to say that two-party competition characterizes the South.

Do Key's criteria for partisan realignment exist in the South? The quick answer is "Yes." The Civil Rights movement, the rise of the Christian Right, and the divisions of the Vietnam War all suggest a period in which voters were quite concerned about a range of issues. Electoral participation expanded during this time period. Although turnout in national elections declined during most of this time, in the South, especially following the Voting Rights Act, higher and higher proportions of both White and African American voters were registering to vote and exercising their right to vote. Pre-existing cleavages among groups of Southern voters shifted, and these shifts persisted over the latter third of the 1900s. Key's four requirements for a partisan realignment appear to have occurred in the South.

The final remaining component of Key's discussion is whether there was a critical election. For Key, a critical election was a clear signal that voters had shifted their allegiance by voting for candidates of the other party and successfully electing them to office. It is difficult to identify a single critical election in the South. Among Peripheral South states, the shift to the Republican party was gradual, slow, and variable. No single election reveals a break-point for these states.

In the Deep South, 1964 is often cited as a critical election year; however, 1972 is probably equally important at the presidential level. For Congress, 1994 could be cited as a critical election. As Havard states, "the vote for Goldwater [in 1964] more closely approximated the 1948 Dixiecrat and 1968 Wallace vote than the emerging Republican urban and traditional vote" (1972, p. 721). The 1964 vote was a deviation from the overall trend in the South. The Southern voters who were switching party identification were not Democratic New Dealers, [and] not racists, but anti–New Dealers who "were 'latent' Republicans kept within the Democratic Party by some kind of pressure" (Sundquist, 1973, p. 257). Sundquist is not very clear about what this "pressure" keeping "latent Republicans" within the Democratic party was, but it was removed by the time of the Second World War, but not at the state and local level. Perhaps this anti–New Deal group simply needed a vehicle for moving, which was provided, for example, in 1948 by the Dixiecrat movement. This argument lacks some force, though, because it is highly likely that the Dixiecrat vote would have been much less if it had not been able to capture the Democratic label on the ballot in several Deep South states.

As Sundquist went on to indicate, an observable trend toward the Republican party did begin as far back as the 1940/1948 period (Sundquist, 1973, p. 259). Converse, Clausen, and Miller (1965) argued that 1948 saw a disruption of this GOP trend, and that the apolitical personality and appeal of Eisenhower helped to reestablish this trend rather dramatically in 1952 and 1956. They further argued that this trend would have receded if it hadn't been for the religious issue in 1960, and the civil rights issue of 1964. The impact of these factors on the voting behavior of Southerners cannot be underestimated. Following this exposition to its conclusion, the civil rights issue was again dominant in 1968, while the personality of George McGovern became a decisive factor in 1972.

The question is, how much of an impact did these occurrences have on the Southern GOP trend? The answer is that they had a varied effect, just as they did in the rest of the country. Voters responded differently in the Peripheral South than they did in the Deep South to these short-run factors. The long-run response is the important one, and it is an overall increase in the Republican vote at all levels in the South.

Taking all four of Key's requirements for partisan realignment, 1968 rather than 1964 emerges as the critical election in the South. Some Peripheral South states had supported Republican presidential candidates in 1952, 1956, and 1960 to one degree or another, but in 1968 only Texas remained in the Democratic column. In the Deep South, 1964 was the first presidential election year that all five states supported the Republican candidate. In 1968, these states could have returned to the Democratic column, but rather than supporting the national Democratic party, they supported the third-party candidacy of George Wallace. Only once since then—1976—has a majority of Deep South states supported the Democratic candidate for president. As stated previously, 1968 was also the first year that substantial numbers of Blacks participated in the electoral process in the South with the accompanying impact of shifting White participation and allegiances. In discussing congressional elections, governor or state legislative races, it is hard to identify that single critical election that Key originally suggested. It is possible to conclude that political realignment has occurred in the South. It occurred as early as 1964 for Blacks. It was occurring by 1968 for Whites, especially for White males.

Even though Barth (1997) argued that "strong Republican presidential candidates have aided candidates in lower-level statewide races who are also on the ticket . . . the decoupling of state elections from presidential elections will, in the South, continue to serve as a barrier to realigning trends"; realignment is occurring (pp. 61–62). The electoral evidence clearly indicates that four states—North Carolina, Tennessee, Virginia, and Florida—are very close to becoming truly competitive two-party states at all levels of government. Texas has been in a holding pattern but may quickly become consistently competitive at all levels with the second term re-election of Republican Governor George W. Bush by an overwhelming margin. If the new moderation of the Republican party in Texas persists, and the party is able to maintain its successful outreach to Hispanic voters, Republicans will be in a competitive position in the state.

Rapid change in the South has not been typical. In 1971, Murphy and Gulliver found that in the Georgia and South Carolina gubernatorial elections, "the Wallace voters of 1968 returned to, and stayed within, the Democratic party in overwhelming numbers" (p. 191). In 1973, Sundquist found that the polls indicated that "most new GOP voters in the South still have not crossed the realignment threshold. As noted in their own eyes they are only 'independents' not yet 'Republicans' " (Sundquist, 1973, p. 347). In 1992, Cotter, Fisher, and Williams found that among native Southern White voters, the Democrats still held a plurality of 6 percent in party identification (1997, p. 71). The answer to this question of whether the GOP will become truly competitive throughout the South is becoming clearer and clearer. The evidence indicates that Republican competitiveness has already occurred in most parts of the South.

If there is one unanswered question, it is what the Republican party will do to sustain the shifts in partisan association and voting behavior. In the past, the early Republican candidates who had contested elections in the South and won office had on the whole been more progressive and moderate than their Democratic counterparts (Key, *Southern Politics*, 1949; Heard, 1952; Havard, 1972). In order to build on these initial successes, some political scientists, such as Sundquist (1973), argued that the quest for new voters could meet with the most success by moving to the political right to attract the large block of Southern "independents"—conservative White Southerners (Sundquist, p. 347). He found that the young were not predominantly liberal or progressive, and that in 1968 voters in their twenties supported Wallace more strongly than any other age group, in and out of the South. With eighteen-to-twenty-one-year-olds voting in higher numbers in future elections as they age, the youth vote will be even more important. As the new, younger generations increase in numbers, influencing partisan preference in the early years can be very important in the long term for a political party's success. Currently, it is the voting group that supported Humphrey, Yarborough, and Gore that is in danger of "dying off," not the Wallaceites.

This early pattern appears to persist today in that the youngest voters in the 1980s were some of the strongest supporters of Republican candidates, whereas younger voters heavily voted for Democrats in the 1990s. Controlling the White House and the perception of the president have become critical factors in influencing party identification, particularly among young voters. Parker and Copa found in Florida that Ronald Reagan was the biggest single influence on party identification during the 1980s, and that Bill Clinton played a similar role in the 1990s (Parker and Copa, 1998). This has been reflected in the recent modest, albeit noticeable, blunting of Republican growth in the South and nationally.

Republican support, which Key had found to be most prevalent in relatively isolated, traditional "Mountain" areas that pre-dated the Civil War, and in urban areas where in-migrants brought their Republicanism with them, has now shifted. By the 1990s Sturrock (1997) was finding that Republican primary votes were coming almost evenly from urban and rural counties in Southern states. The increase in Republican voting is widespread across states and the South.

The nationalization, yet continued differentiation of Southern politics is also being reflected in findings that "in 1988 and 1992, the South experienced more class bias in voting than did the non-South"—levels of difference that approximated those of forty years earlier (Cotter, Fisher, and Williams, 1997, p. 75). Based on 1996 exit poll data on Southern voters, Black (1998) argues that if you remove African Americans and Whites who identify themselves as Religious Right voters, other Whites break along income lines in their identification as Republicans or Democrats. This finding is more pronounced in the Deep South than in the Peripheral South. Higher-income men and women identify with the Republican party, while low-income men and women are more likely to identify as Democrats. Somewhat surprisingly, higher-income men are slightly less likely to be Republican than higher-income women. Middle-income men are more likely to identify as Republicans, and middle-income women as Democrats (Black, 1998). Gender, along with income, plays an important role in party preference.

In 2000, another presidential election will occur. There will be no incumbent president in 2000, and there is a strong likelihood that both the Republicans and the Democrats will nominate Southerners to lead their tickets. The South is likely to continue its Republican support at the presidential level.

In the U.S. Senate, thirty-three Senate seats will be up for election in 2000—nineteen Republican seats and fourteen Democratic seats. Five Southern senate Seats are among those to be elected—one Democrat (Robb in Virginia), and four Republicans (Mack in Florida, Lott in Mississippi, Frist in Tennessee, and Hutchison in Texas). Robb is considered very vulnerable. He survived a close race in 1994 and will most likely face popular, former Governor George Allen in 2000. Three of the four Republicans—Lott, Frist, and Hutchison—are considered to be safe in their re-election bids. In Florida, Connie

Mack is retiring, so the seat is open. The party candidates and the strength of the presidential candidates in the state will determine whether the Republicans retain this seat. Potentially, the Republicans could have a net gain of the Virginia Senate seat in the South in 2000, increasing their majority in the South. At worst, the 2000 election could result in a net loss of one Republican Senate seat in the South, if the Democrats hold the Virginia seat and pick up the open Florida seat. Nationally, the number of retirements and open seats may determine whether the Republicans will lose a seat or two in the 2000 election. Republicans will retain their majority in the Senate and might even increase it, depending upon candidates in open seats, which other incumbents choose to retire, and how well the presidential candidates perform.

The entire U.S. House of Representatives will be elected. Since the vast majority of incumbents are re-elected each year, only the margins will be affected. However, the Republicans have a small majority in the House. In the South, the Republicans have essentially maximized their ability to capture House districts. Some members of the House are finding themselves confronting their pledges in 1994 to limit their terms in office to six years. As part of the 1994 Republican Contract with America, new House members pledged to retire in the year 2000. Most who pledged to do so, have done so, but several have not. If Democrats can successfully use the "pledge" against Republican candidates, this may shift partisan control of some seats. Democrats will mount a strong campaign to recruit strong candidates in an effort to regain the majority in the House. Again, the presidential candidates can influence marginal races for the House, but there is a strong likelihood that the Republican party will lose control of the House in the 2000 election, and may even lose a seat or two in the South.

In 1999, three states elected governors, including both Louisiana and Mississippi in the South. Incumbents typically do well when seeking re-election. In Louisiana, Mike Foster experienced a divisive primary in 1995, but he was supported by the strong conservative Christian Right in the state. By 1999, Foster enjoyed broad support for his conservative, limited government, pro-business approach to the state. He was re-elected with 62 percent of the vote. In Mississippi there was no incumbent governor although Republicans held the governor's office going into the election. With scandal swirling around the out-going Republican governor, and both Republican and Democratic challengers pursuing conservative campaigns on the issues, Democrat Ronnie Musgrove garnered more votes than Republican Mike Parker. Because neither won a majority of the votes and a majority of the state legislative house districts, the Democratic controlled Mississippi house of representatives elected Musgrove governor.

Eleven governors will be elected nationally in 2000. Seven of the seats are currently held by Democrats and four by Republicans. North Carolina is the only Southern governorship open in 2000. Incumbent Democrat Jim Hunt is prohibited from seeking another term. Although this seat will be competitive with both parties fielding strong candidates, it is probable that the Democrats will retain the seat given the statewide trend away from the Republican party in recent elections, unlike most of North Carolina's neighbors. Other incumbents appear to be strongly favored to win re-election.

At the state legislative level, Barone, Lilley, and DeFranco have observed, "Two verities of twentieth century American politics, wealth and location, will continue to define American politics early in the twenty-first century—at least at the state level. Republicans remain the party of wealth—in some states by a staggering margin" (1998, p. 1). The Republican party is the party of choice of wealthier Americans in all regions no matter the size of the state or the nature of its economy. In eleven states the state legislative districts that elect Republicans are 30–50 percent wealthier than districts that elect Democrats, including the Deep Southern states of Georgia, Alabama, Louisiana, Mississippi, and South Carolina, and the Peripheral state of Texas. In the fifteen states where Republican districts are 20–30 percent wealthier, North Carolina and Tennessee appear. Only in Arkansas and Florida is the difference small, and only in Virginia in the South are the districts even in terms of wealth. Wealth and class have emerged as key characteristics of the Republican growth in the Deep South in particular. Whites, who have traditionally controlled the wealth of the rural South, and the burgeoning growth of new urban, white-collar centers, have combined with partisan identification in the Republican party.

The second factor mentioned by Barone, Lilley, and DeFranco relates to location. Even with the rapid growth of the South as a whole, it remains a strongly rural region of the country. Of the state legislative districts in the South, 41 percent are rural, 26 percent are urban, and 29 percent are suburban. Republicans and Democrats evenly split legislative districts that are primarily rural (48 percent Republican and 49 percent Democratic), whereas Republicans represent 55 percent of suburban districts and Democrats represent 69 percent of urban districts. Overall, Democrats hold 52 percent of the legislative districts in the South compared to 45 percent for Republicans (1998, p. 2).

As the South continues to lose rural areas as the suburbs of urban centers spill across the countryside in virtually every Southern state, the political power will shift as districts are redrawn. In six Southern states—Alabama, Florida, Louisiana, South Carolina, Texas, and Tennessee—Republicans do best in the suburbs. In only one state— Florida—do the Democrats do best in the suburbs. In three states—Tennessee, Texas, and Virginia—the Democrats do best in the urban districts, whereas Republicans do best in urban districts in no Southern states (Barone, Lilley, and DeFranco, 1998, p. 2).

Redistricting in the wake of the 2000 Census will be very important for future control of state legislatures. If Democrats continue to control state legislative houses, they will be confronted with redistricting states where they will have to choose how many rural districts will be redrawn as suburban districts, and thus become more likely to elect Republican representatives in the 2002 elections. Republican control of state legislative houses, or growth to the point of being able to seriously block Democratic action, will increase in 2000, and continue to do so in succeeding years since the trends are for continued growth in wealth and suburban residence. The twenty-first century will witness the completion of the realignment of the South.

Cotter, Fisher, and Williams (1997) further found that "overall, our results reveal a South that is generally becoming both less and less biased in its politics and more and more like the rest of the country" (1997, p. 75). Politically, the South has experienced a partisan realignment among both African Americans and native Whites. While the South, like much of the world, has become more like the rest of the country through a combination of mass media marketing and advertising, and the in-migration of people from other parts of the country and abroad, it still retains much of its traditional culture and values. At the same time, the ascendance of Southerners in both the White House and the Congress has continued the influence of the region on the political agenda and the policy options that have shaped, and will continue to shape, the national scene.

# Bibliography

*America at the Polls.* Washington, D.C.: Congressional Quarterly Service, 1996.

Anderson, R. Bruce. "Electoral Competition and Southern State Legislatures: The Dynamics of Change." In *Southern Politics and Elections,* ed. Robert P. Steed, Lawrence Moreland, and Tod A. Baker, 165–181. Tuscaloosa: University of Alabama Press, 1997.

Ayers, H. Brandt, and Thomas H. Naylor, eds. *You Can't Eat Magnolias.* New York: McGraw-Hill Book Co., 1972.

Barone, Michael, William Lilley III, and Laurence J. DeFranco. *State Legislative Elections: Voting Patterns and Demographics.* Washington, D.C.: Congressional Quarterly, Inc., 1998.

Barth, Jay. "The Impact of Election Timing on Republican Trickle-Down in the South." In *Southern Politics and Elections,* ed. Robert P. Steed, Lawrence Moreland, and Tod A. Baker, 52–62. Tuscaloosa: University of Alabama Press, 1997.

Beachler, Donald W. "Redistricting and Nationalization: Southern House Elections in the 1990s." *Southeastern Political Review* 24, no. 4, December 1996: 777–788.

Beck, Paul Allen. "Party Realignment in America: The View from the States." In *Party Realignment and State Politics,* ed.

Maureen Moakley, 259–278. Columbus: Ohio State University Press, 1992.

Beck, Paul Allen. "A Socialization Theory of Partisan Realignment." In *The Politics of Future Citizens,* ed. Richard G. Niemi. San Francisco: Jossey-Bass, 1974.

Black, Earl, and Merle Black. *Politics and Society in the South.* Cambridge, MA: Harvard University Press, 1987.

Black, Earl, and Merle Black. *The Vital South: How Presidents Are Elected.* Cambridge, MA: Harvard University Press, 1992.

Black, Merle. Roundtable discussion. Southern Political Science Association, Atlanta, GA, October 30, 1998.

Black, Merle, and Earl Black. "Party Institutionalization in the American South: The Growth of Contested Republican Primaries." Paper delivered at the Annual Meeting of the Southern Political Science Association. Atlanta, GA, October 28–31, 1998.

*The Book of the States.* Chicago, IL: The Council of State Governments, 1950–1972.

Brady, David, John F. Cogan, and Douglas Rivers. *The 1996 House Elections: Reaffirming the Conservative Trend.* Stanford, CA: Hoover Institution, 1997.

Bullock, Charles S., III. "Regional Realignment from an Officeholding Perspective." *The Journal of Politics* 50, no. 3, August 1998: 553–574.

Bullock, Charles S., III, and Mark J. Rozell, eds. *The New Politics of the Old South.* Lanham, MD: Rowman and Littlefield Publishers, Inc., 1998.

Burnham, Walter Dean. "Critical Realignment: Dead or Alive?" In *The End of Realignment: Interpreting American Electoral Eras,* ed. Byron E. Schafer, 101–140. Madison: University of Wisconsin Press, 1991.

Carmines, Edward, and James Stimson. *Issue Evaluation: Race and the Transformation of American Politics.* Princeton, NJ: Princeton University Press, 1991.

Coleman, John J. "The Importance of Being Republican: Forecasting Party Fortunes in House Midterm Elections." *The Journal of Politics* 59, no. 2, May 1997: 497–519.

*Congressional Quarterly Almanac.* Vols. 24, 26, 28. Washington, D.C.: Congressional Quarterly Service, 1968, 1970, 1972.

*Congressional Quarterly Weekly Reports.* Nov. 7, 1992, Dec. 21, 1996, Jan. 18, 1997. Washington, D.C.: Congressional Quarterly Service.

Converse, Philip E., Aage R. Clausen, and Warren E. Miller. "Electoral Myth and Reality: The 1964 Election." *American Political Science Review* 59, no. 2, June 1965: 321–336.

Cook, Rhodes. "Election End Results, County by County." *Congressional Quarterly Weekly Report,* December 21, 1996: 3443–3447.

Cook, Rhodes. "Even with Higher Vote, Clinton Remains Minority President." *Congressional Quarterly Weekly Report,* January 18, 1997: 185–187.

Cook, Rhodes. "Thinnest of Margins Shows Country's Great Divide." *Congressional Quarterly Weekly Report,* February 15, 1997: 441–442.

Cooke, Jacob E., ed. *The Federalist.* New York: The World Publishing Company, 1961.

Cosman, Bernard. *Five States for Goldwater: Continuity and Change in Southern Presidential Voting Patterns.* University: University of Alabama Press, 1967.

Cosman, Bernard. "Presidential Republicanism in the South, 1960." *The Journal of Politics* 24, no. 2, May 1962: 303–322.

Cotter, Patrick R., Samuel H. Fisher, and Felita T. Williams. "Changes in the Composition of Political Activists: 1952–1992." In *Southern Politics and Elections,* ed. Robert P. Steed, Lawrence Moreland, and Tod A. Baker, 63–77. Tuscaloosa: University of Alabama Press, 1997.

Cox, Edward F. "The Measurement of Party Strength." *Western Political Quarterly* 13, no. 4, December 1960: 1022–1042.

David, Paul T. "How Can an Index of Party Competition Best Be Derived?" *The Journal of Politics* 34, no. 2, May 1972: 632–638.

David, Paul T. *Party Strength in the United States.* Charlottesville: University Press of Virginia, 1972.

Eamon, Thomas. "Dixie Versus the Nonsouthern Megastates in American Presidential Politics." In *Southern Politics and Elections,* ed. Robert P. Steed, Lawrence Moreland, and Tod A. Baker, 109–130. Tuscaloosa: University of Alabama Press, 1997.

Epstein, David, and Sharyn O'Halloran. "A Social Science Approach to Race, Redistricting, and Representation." *American Political Science Review* 93, no. 2, March 1999: 187–191.

Ewing, Cortez A. M. "Southern Governors." *The Journal of Politics* 10, no. 2, May 1948: 385–410.

Gatlin, Douglas S. "Toward a Functionalist Theory of Political Parties: Inter-Party Competition in North Carolina." In *Approaches to the Study of Party Organizations,* ed. W. J. Crotty, 217–246. Boston, MA: Allyn and Bacon, 1968.

Golembiewski, Robert T. "A Taxonomic Approach to State Political Party Strength." *Western Political Quarterly* 11, no. 3, September 1958: 494–513.

Guide to U.S. Elections. 1994. Washington, D.C.: Congressional Quarterly Inc.

Guth, James L. "God's Own Party." *Christianity Today* 110, February 17, 1993: 172.

Havard, William C. *The Changing Politics of the South.* Baton Rouge: Louisiana State University Press, 1972.

Heard, Alexander. *A Two-Party South?* Chapel Hill: University of North Carolina Press, 1952.

Huckshorn, Robert J. *Political Parties in America.* North Scituate, MA: Duxbury Press, 1980.

Hunter, Floyd. *Community Power Structure.* Chapel Hill: University of North Carolina Press, 1953.

Jackson, Robert A. "The Mobilization of the U.S. State Electorate in the 1988 and 1990 Elections." *The Journal of Politics* 59, no. 2, May 1997: 520–537.

Jacob, Herbert, and Kenneth N. Vines, eds. *Politics in the American States.* Boston: Little, Brown and Co., 1971.

Jewell, Malcolm E. *Legislative Representation in the Contemporary South.* Durham, NC: Duke University Press, 1967.

Kazee, Thomas A. "North Carolina: Conservatism, Traditionalism, and the GOP." In *The New Politics of the Old South,* ed. Charles S. Bullock III, and Mark J. Rozell, 141–166. Lanham, MD: Rowman and Littlefield Publishers, Inc., 1998.

Key, V. O., Jr. *American State Politics.* New York: Alfred Knopf, 1956.

Key, V. O., Jr. *Southern Politics in State and Nation.* New York: Vintage Books, 1949.

Kuklinski, James H., Michael D. Cobb, and Martin Gilens. "Racial Attitudes and the 'New South.' " *The Journal of Politics* 59, no. 2, May 1997: 323–349.

Lublin, David. "Racial Redistricting and African-American Representation: A Critique of 'Do Majority-Minority Districts Maximize Substantive Black Representation in Congress?' " *American Political Science Review* 93, no. 2, March 1999: 183–186.

Matthews, Donald R., and James W. Prothro. *Negroes and the New Southern Politics.* New York: Harcourt, Brace and World, 1966.

Matthews, Donald R., and James W. Prothro. "Southern Images of Political Parties: An Analysis of White and Negro Attitudes." *The Journal of Politics* 26, no. 1, February 1964: 82–112.

McLachlan, John M., and Joe S. Floyd, Jr. *This Changing South.* Gainesville: University of Florida Press, 1956.

Miller, Warren E., and J. Merrill Shanks. *The New American Voter.* Cambridge: Harvard University Press, 1996.

Murphy, Reg, and Hal Gulliver. *The Southern Strategy.* New York: Charles Scribner's Sons, 1971.

National Conference of State Legislatures. "Democratic Share of State Legislative Seats, 1960–96," NCSLnet (*http://www.ncsl.org/programs/legman/elect/DEMSHARE.HTM*), Dec. 5, 1996.

National Conference of State Legislatures. "Partisan Control of State Legislatures, 1960–96," NCSLnet (*http://www.ncsl.org/programs/legman/elect/partycontpost1.gif*), Dec. 5, 1996.

National Conference of State Legislatures. "1998 Election Analysis," NCSLnet (*http://www.ncsl.org/statevote98/analysis1998.htm*), Nov. 4, 1998.

Nichols, Stephen M., and Paul Allen Beck. "Reversing the Decline: Voter Turnout in the 1992 Election." In *Democracy's Feast: Elections in America*, ed. Herbert F. Weisber, 29–71. Chatham, NJ: Chatham House Publishers, Inc., 1995.

*The 1968 Elections: A Summary Report.* Washington, D.C.: Republican Party National Committee Research Division, 1970.

Parker, Suzanne L., and Juan C. Copa. "The Evolution of Party Identification among Whites, Blacks, and Hispanics in Florida, 1979–1997." Paper presented at the 1998 Southern Political Science Association meeting, Atlanta, GA. October 28–31, 1998.

Pfeiffer, David G. "The Measurement of Inter-Party Competition and Systematic Stability." *American Political Science Review* 61, no. 2, June 1967: 457–467.

Phillips, Kevin. *The Emerging Republican Majority.* New York: Doubleday and Co., 1969.

Ranney, Austin. "Parties in State Politics." In *Politics in the American States: A Comparative Analysis,* ed. Herbert Jacobs and Kenneth Vines, 82–121. Boston, MA: Little, Brown and Co., 1971.

Ranney, Austin, and Willmoor Kendall. "The American Party System." *American Political Science Review* 48, no. 2, June 1954: 477–485.

Ransome, Coleman B. *The Office of Governor in the South.* University: University of Alabama Press, 1951.

Ransome, Coleman B. "Political Leadership in the Governor's Office." *The Journal of Politics* 26, no. 1, February 1964: 197–221.

Rapaport, Ronald B. "Partisanship Change in a Candidate-Centered Era." *The Journal of Politics* 59, no. 1, February 1997: 185–199.

Riedel, James A., ed. *New Perspectives in State and Local Politics.* Waltham, MA: Xerox College Publishing, 1971.

Rozell, Mark J. "Virginia: The New Politics of the Old Dominion." In *Politics in the New South: Republicanism, Race, and Leadership in the Twentieth Century,* ed. Richard K. Scher, 123–140. Armonk, NY: M.E. Sharpe, 1998.

Scammon, Richard M., ed. *America Votes: I–IX.* New York: Macmillan, Co., 1956–1970.

Scammon, Richard M., Alice McGillivray, and Rhodes Cook, eds. *America Votes: A Handbook of Contemporary American Election Statistics, X–XV.* Washington, D.C.: Congressional Quarterly, Inc., 1974–1996.

Schafer, Byron E. *The End of Realignment: Interpreting American Electoral Eras.* Madison: University of Wisconsin Press, 1991.

Schattschneider, E. E. *Party Government.* New York: Farrar and Rinehart, 1942.

Scher, Richard K., ed. *Politics in the New South: Republicanism, Race, and Leadership in the Twentieth Century.* 2nd ed. Armonk, NY: M.E. Sharpe, 1997.

Schlesinger, Joseph A. "A Two-Dimensional Scheme for Classifying the States According to Degree of Inter-Party Competition." *American Political Science Review* 49, no. 4, December 1955: 1120–1128.

Scicchitano, Michael J., and Richard K. Scher. "Florida: Political Change, 1950– 1996." In *Politics in the New South: Republicanism, Race, and Leadership in the Twentieth Century,* 2nd ed., Richard K. Scher, 227–244. Armonk, NY: M.E. Sharpe, 1997.

Seagull, Louis Martin. "Southern Republicanism: Party Competition in the American South, 1940–1968." Ph.D. Dissertation, The University of Chicago, 1971.

Shannon, Jasper B. "Presidential Politics in the South." *The Journal of Politics* 10, no. 3, August 1946: 464–490.

Smith, Frank E. *Look Away from Dixie.* Baton Rouge: Louisiana State University Press, 1965.

*State Administrative Officials Classified by Functions.* Lexington, KY: The Council of State Governments, 1957–1969.

*State Elective Officials and the Legislatures.* Chicago, IL: The Council of State Governments, 1957–1971.

*The State of the South 1998.* Chapel Hill, NC: Manpower Development Corporation. (*http://www.mdcinc.org*).

Steed, Robert P., Lawrence W. Moreland, and Tod A. Baker, eds. *Southern Politics and Elections.* Tuscaloosa: University of Alabama Press, 1997.

Strong, Donald. "Further Reflections on Southern Politics." *The Journal of Politics* 33, no. 2, May 1971: 239–256.

Strong, Donald. *The 1952 Presidential Election in the South.* University, AL: Bureau of Public Administration, 1953.

Strong, Donald. *Urban Republicanism in the South.* University, AL: Bureau of Public Administration, 1960.

Sturrock, David E. "Out of the Phone Booth: Republican Primaries in the Deep South." In *Southern Politics and Elections,* ed. Robert P. Steed, Lawrence W. Moreland, and Tod A. Baker, 95–108. Tuscaloosa: University of Alabama Press, 1997.

Sundquist, James L. *Dynamics of the Party System: Alignment and Realignment of Political Parties in the United States.* Washington, D.C.: The Brookings Institution, 1973.

Tindall, George Brown. *The Disruption of the Solid South.* Athens: University of Georgia Press, 1972.

Tindall, George Brown. *The Emergence of the New South*. Baton Rouge: Louisiana State University Press, 1967.

U.S. Bureau of the Census. *Congressional District Atlas*. Washington, D.C.: Government Printing Office, 1960–1973.

U.S. Bureau of the Census. *General Population Characteristics*. Washington, D.C.: Government Printing Office, 1970.

U.S. Bureau of the Census. "Percent Reported Voted and Registered by Race, Hispanic Origin and Gender: November 1964 to Present." *Current Population Survey*, (*http://www.census.gov/population*), October 17, 1997.

U.S. Bureau of the Census. *Population of the United States*. Washington, D.C.: Government Printing Office, 1920, 1950, 1960, 1970.

U.S. House of Representatives. *Statistics of the Presidential and Congressional Elections*. Washington, D.C.: Government Printing Office, 1950, 1952–1954, 1962–1970.

Weeks, O. Douglas. "The South in National Politics." *The Journal of Politics* 26, no. 1, February 1964: 221–241.

Wekkin, Gary D. "Arkansas: Electoral Competition in the 1990s." In *Politics in the New South: Republicanism, Race, and Leadership in the Twentieth Century*, 2nd ed. Richard K. Scher, 185–204. Armonk, NY: M.E. Sharpe, 1997.

White, Clifton F. *Suite 3505*. New Rochelle, NY: Arlington House, 1967.

White, Theodore H. *The Making of the President*. New York: Atheneum Publishers, 1960, 1964, 1968, 1972.

Wilson, James Q. *American Government*. 5th ed. Lexington, MA: D.C. Heath and Company, 1992.

Wrighton, J. Mark, and Peverill Squire. "Uncontested Seats and Electoral Competition for the U.S. House of Representatives Over Time." *The Journal of Politics* 59, no. 2, May 1997: 452–468.

**COURT CASES**

*Hays v. Louisiana*, 839 F. Supp. 1188 (W. D. La. 1993)

*Miller v. Johnson*, 115 S. Ct. 2475 (1995)

*Shaw v. Hunt*, 115 S. Ct. 2639 (1998)

*Shaw v. Reno*, 113 S. Ct. 2816 (1993)

*Thornburg v. Gingles*, 478 U.S. 30, 36–37 (1986)

# Index

African American voters, 21, 28, 48, 49, 55, 62, 97, 103, 111–12; voting, 22, 63, 99, 111, 119–20

Alabama, 13, 15, 114, 129, 130; competition indices, 91, 96, 99, 101, 107; governor, 65, 73–75, 79; presidential politics, 25, 30; state legislature, 81, 86, 88–89; U.S. House, 51, 53–54; U.S. Senate, 44–45

Allen, George, 78, 127

Arkansas, 13, 15, 112, 129; competition indices, 92, 96, 99, 101, 106–7; governor, 68, 73–74, 79; presidential politics, 25, 30, 36; state legislature, 86, 88, 89; U.S. House, 53, 54, 61; U.S. Senate, 40, 45, 46, 48–50

Armey, Dick, 114

Baker, Howard, 43

Barnes, Roy, 75–76

Bayh, Evan, 45

Beasley, David, 75, 77

Bishop, Sanford, 64

Bradley, Bill, 28

Breaux, James, 45

Brock, Bill, 43

Bumpers, Dale, 71

Bunning, Jim, 45

Bush, George, 18, 28, 30, 32, 36, 80

Bush, George W., 28, 36, 74, 78, 125

Bush, Jeb, 74

Byrd, Harry, Jr., 44

Byrd machine, 5, 71

Calloway, Bo, 73

Carter, Jimmy, 18, 22, 27, 33, 44, 75, 80

Christian Right. *See* Religious Right

Civil War, 1, 13, 15, 111

Clinton, Bill, 18, 27, 29, 30, 32–33, 45, 76, 80, 110, 112, 116, 119, 126

Coats, Dan, 45

Competition Index, 94, 97; categories, 93–94, 97; gubernatorial, 100; state legislative, 106–7

Composite B Index, 97, 100

Contract with America. *See* Republican Revolution of 1994

Coverdell, Paul, 45, 50

Cramer, Bill, 71

Critical election, 120, 123–25

D'Amato, Alfonse, 45

Deal, Nathan, 64

Deep South, 13, 15, 110, 114, 124–25, 127, 129; competition indices, 97, 100–101, 106–7; governor, 73–74, 78; presidential politics, 21, 32–33; U.S. House, 50–55, 57, 59, 61–62; U.S. Senate, 40, 43–46, 49

DeLay, Tom, 114

Dixiecrats, 19, 21, 33, 43, 124

Dole, Bob, 28, 30, 36, 59, 76, 116, 119

Dukakis, Michael, 27

Dunn, Winfield, 71

Edwards, John, 46

Eisenhower, Dwight, 21, 53, 124

Electoral votes, 23–27, 110

Faircloth, Lauch, 46, 49

Faubus, Orville, 68

First-time voters, 29, 31–32

Fitzgerald, Peter, 45

Florida, 13, 110, 112, 125, 127, 129, 130; competition indices, 92, 96, 101, 104, 106; governor, 68, 71, 73, 74, 79; presidential politics, 21, 23, 25, 36–38; state legislature, 81, 86, 88, 89; U.S. House, 51, 53, 54, 61, 65; U.S. Senate, 43, 46

Ford, Gerald, 28

Ford, Wendell, 45

Fordice, Kirk, 75, 79

Foster, Mike, 75, 77, 79, 128

Frist, Bill, 127

Gender gap, 116, 127

Georgia, 13, 15, 114, 125, 129; competition indices, 92, 96, 99, 101, 106–7; governor, 73, 75–76, 79; presidential politics, 23, 25, 36–38; state legislature, 81, 86, 88, 89; U.S. House, 50–51, 53, 54, 57, 61, 62, 64; U.S. Senate, 40, 45

Gerrymandering, 62, 63

Gingrich, Newt, 65, 114

Glenn, John, 45

Godwin, Mills, 71

Goldwater, Barry, 11, 21, 22, 28, 32, 43–44, 51–52, 55, 97, 100–101, 111, 122, 124

Gore, Al, 28

Gore, Al, Sr., 43, 126

Graham, Bob, 46

Gurney, Ed, 43

Hastert, Dennis, 114
*Hays v. Louisiana,* 64
Helms, Jesse, 43, 73
Hispanic voters, 48, 62, 111, 112, 125
Hodges, James, 75
Hollings, Fritz, 45
Holshouser, James, 71, 73
Holton, Linwood, 71
Hooker, John J., 71
Howell, Henry, 71
Humphrey, Hubert, 27, 126
Hunt, Jim, 74, 129
Hutchinson, Tim, 45
Hutchison, Kay Bailey, 127

Income and wealth, 55, 67, 109, 129
Indices of party competition, 91; David, 93, 97; Lag Score, 103–7; Pfeiffer, 92–93; Ranney, 91–92

James, Fob, 75
Johnson, Lyndon, 18, 21–22, 27, 28, 43, 80, 111, 122

Key, V. O., Jr., 11–12, 15, 120, 124–25
King, Robert High, 71
Kirk, Claude, 71

Lag Score, 103–7
Lincoln, Blanche, 46
Livingston, Bob, 114
Lott, Trent, 114, 127
Louisiana, 13, 112, 114, 128–29, 130; competition indices, 92, 96, 99, 101, 107; governor, 68, 73, 74, 75, 77, 79; presidential poli-
tics, 25, 30; state legislature, 81, 86, 89; U.S. House, 53–54, 57, 59, 61, 63; U.S. Senate, 40, 45

Mack, Connie, 127–28
Maddox, Lester, 73
Madison, James, 8–10
Majority-minority districts, 61–64, 80, 103, 113, 114–15
McGovern, George, 27, 124
McKinney, Cynthia, 64
Megastates, 110
*Miller v. Johnson,* 64
Miller, Zell, 75
Millner, Guy, 75
Mississippi, 13, 114, 127, 128–29; competition indices, 92, 96, 99, 101, 107; governor, 68, 74–76, 79; presidential politics, 23, 25, 37; state legislature, 81, 86, 89; U.S. House, 51, 53–54, 57; U.S. Senate, 40, 44, 45
Mondale, Walter, 27
Moseley-Braun, Carole, 45
Mountain Republicans, 15, 51, 53, 54, 73, 104, 111, 127
Musgrove, Ronnie, 75, 79, 129

Nationalization of Southern politics, 2, 17
New Deal Democratic coalition, 29
Nixon, Richard, 32, 54, 63, 80, 111, 122
North Carolina, 13, 15, 112, 113, 125, 129; competition indices, 92, 96, 99, 101, 104, 106; governor, 68, 73, 74, 76, 79; presidential poli-

tics, 19, 22, 25, 38; state
legislature, 81, 86, 88–89;
U.S. House, 50–51, 53, 54,
61–64; U.S. Senate, 43, 45,
46, 49

Parker, Mike, 79, 129
Partisan competition. *See*
Two-party competition
Partisan realignment, 2, 12,
15, 17, 31, 37, 115, 123,
125, 130; criteria for, 120
Party competition. *See* Two-
party competition
Party registration, 7, 23, 36,
37, 48, 121–22
Peripheral South, 13, 15, 110,
124–25, 127, 129; competition indices, 97, 99–101,
106–7; governor, 68, 73–74,
76, 78; presidential politics,
21–22, 32–33; state legislature, 89; U.S. House, 51–55,
57, 59, 61; U.S. Senate, 40,
43–46, 49
Perot, Ross, 29
Political cleavages, 122
Political parties: characteristics of American, 4–5; definition, 3; functions of, 4;
ideology, 6–7; influence of
process, 5; leadership, 6–7;
organization, 5
Post-Industrial/post-Party
politics, 55
Presidential Republicanism,
11, 15–16, 36–37
Primaries and primary elections, 5–6; participation in,
36–37, 49, 112, 127; presi-

dential, 36; senatorial, 46,
48
Pryor, David, 46

Race, 19, 21–22, 40, 55,
63–64, 68, 71, 111–15. *See
also* Redistricting
Reagan, Ronald, 28, 31–32,
44, 63, 80, 99, 126
Reconstruction, 50, 119, 123
Redistricting, 59, 61–64, 80,
103, 113, 114–15, 130
Regional voting patterns,
25–27, 30, 44–45, 48–50,
65, 110, 114
Religion, 31, 116–19
Religious Right, 75, 77–78,
118, 120, 123, 127–28
Republican "L," 45, 49–50
Republican Revolution of
1994, 11, 18, 55, 57, 81,
87–88, 106, 124, 127–28
Richards, Ann, 78
Robb, Charles, 127
Rockefeller, Winthrop, 68, 71
Roemer, Buddy, 77

Schumer, Charles, 45
Scott, William, 43
*Shaw v. Hunt*, 64
*Shaw v. Reno*, 63
Shelby, Richard, 44–45
Siegelman, Don, 75
Solid South, 17; Democratic,
19, 23, 27; Republican,
21–22, 24, 27, 30, 32, 54
South Carolina, 13, 114, 125,
129, 130; competition indi-
ces, 92, 96, 99, 100, 101,
106, 107; governor, 73,
74–75, 79; presidential poli-

tics, 25, 38; state legislature, 81, 86, 88, 89; U.S. House, 53, 54; U.S. Senate, 40, 43, 44, 45

Southern: defined, 13; identity, 1, 67; role of Civil War, 2

Southern Democracy, 67

Southern Republicanism, 11, 32

Southern Strategy, 11, 32, 63, 101, 111–12, 113, 122

State legislative elections: off-years, 81, 86–87; presidential years, 80, 86–87

Stennis, John, 112

Tennessee, 13, 15, 19, 112, 125, 127, 129, 130; competition indices, 92, 96, 99, 101, 104, 106, 107; governor, 73–74; presidential politics, 21, 25, 36–38; state legislature, 81, 86, 88, 89; U.S. House, 50, 51, 53, 54, 55, 57, 65; U.S. Senate, 43, 45

Terry, Mary Sue, 78

Texas, 13, 110, 125, 127, 129, 130; competition indices, 92, 96, 99, 101, 106–7; governor, 74, 78; presidential politics, 19, 22, 23, 25, 36–38; state legislature, 81, 86, 88, 89; U.S. House, 51, 53, 54, 55, 57, 61; U.S. Senate, 43, 45

Theodore, Nick, 77

Third-party candidates, 16, 28, 29, 32, 33, 40, 92, 94–95

Thornburg v. Gingles, 61

Thurmond, Strom, 21, 43, 100

Tower, John, 43

Trickle down effect, 23, 89, 113, 123

Truman, Harry, 22, 79

Two-party competition, 8, 10, 13, 17, 68, 79, 97, 100, 123; presidential, 33, 36, 95–97, 110; senatorial, 40; state legislative, 86–89

Urban Republicans, 15, 21, 51, 53–55, 73, 102–3, 106, 111, 127

Virginia, 5, 13, 15, 125, 127, 129, 130; competition indices, 92, 96, 99, 100–102; governor, 68, 71, 73, 74, 76–78; presidential politics, 19, 21, 25; state legislature, 81, 86, 89; U.S. House, 51, 53–54, 55, 56–57, 61; U.S. Senate, 40, 43–44

Voinovich, John, 45

Voter turnout, 29, 112, 121–22

Voting Rights Act of 1965, 32, 48, 55, 61, 97, 99, 111, 119, 120–23

Wallace, George, 22, 32, 111–12, 124, 125–26

Warner, John, 77

Watson, Albert, 53

Watt, Mel, 64

White Democrats, 15, 21, 40, 55, 62, 64; voters, 28, 48–49, 51–52, 62, 73, 103, 111–12, 119–20

Women's movement, 116

Young, Andrew, 54

## About the Author

TERREL L. RHODES is Special Assistant to the Provost for Assessment and Associate Professor of Political Science at the University of North Carolina, Charlotte. Professor Rhodes has published extensively in edited collections and scholarly journals.